Dialectical Behavior Therapy for Eating Disorders

This book explores the application of dialectical behavior therapy (DBT) in treating eating disorders (EDs), highlighting its theoretical and clinical significance alongside emerging empirical support theoretical and clinical relevance, as well as burgeoning empirical support, for the treatment of EDs.

Originally developed for patients with borderline personality disorder, DBT recognizes that maladaptive, impulsive behaviors often arise from attempts to manage intense emotions and focuses on cultivating adaptive skills for better emotional self-regulation. With robust evidence linking emotion regulation difficulties to eating disorder symptoms, research increasingly supports DBT's effectiveness for conditions such as bulimia nervosa and binge eating disorder. The contributors to this volume are experts in the field who have decades of clinical and research experience in DBT and eating disorders and they delve into the nuances of adapting DBT for patients with complex presentations and comorbid conditions, reflecting the latest advancements in this vital area of therapy.

The chapters in this book were originally published as a special issue of *Eating Disorders: The Journal of Treatment and Prevention.*

Tiffany A. Brown is Assistant Professor in the Department of Psychological Sciences at Auburn University and Co-Director of the Auburn Eating Disorders Clinic, AL.

Lucene Wisniewski is the founder of Center for Evidence Based Treatment, and an Adjunct Assistant Professor in the Department of Psychological Sciences at Case Western Reserve University, Cleveland, OH.

Leslie K. Anderson is Clinical Professor and Assistant Clinical Director of the University of California San Diego Eating Disorders Center for Treatment and Research, CA.

Dialectical Behavior Therapy for Eating Disorders

State of the Research and Future Directions

Edited by
Tiffany A. Brown, Lucene Wisniewski and Leslie K. Anderson

Routledge
Taylor & Francis Group
NEW YORK AND LONDON

First published 2025
by Routledge
4 Park Square, Milton Park, Abingdon, Oxon OX14 4RN

and by Routledge
605 Third Avenue, New York, NY 10158

Routledge is an imprint of the Taylor & Francis Group, an informa business

British Library Cataloguing in Publication Data
A catalogue record for this book is available from the British Library

ISBN13: 978-1-003-86416-5 (hbk)
ISBN13: 978-1-003-86417-2 (pbk)
ISBN13: 978-1-003-60762-5 (ebk)

DOI: 10.4324/9781003607625

Typeset in Minion Pro
by Newgen Publishing UK

Publisher's Note
The publisher accepts responsibility for any inconsistencies that may have arisen during the conversion of this book from journal articles to book chapters, namely the inclusion of journal terminology.

Disclaimer
Every effort has been made to contact copyright holders for their permission to reprint material in this book. The publishers would be grateful to hear from any copyright holder who is not here acknowledged and will undertake to rectify any errors or omissions in future editions of this book.

Contents

Citation Information

The chapters in this book were originally published in the *Eating Disorders: Journal of Treatment and Prevention*, volume 28, issue 2 (2020). When citing this material, please use the original page numbering for each article, as follows:

Chapter 1

Dialectical Behavior Therapy for Eating Disorders: State of the Research and New Directions
Tiffany A. Brown, Lucene Wisniewski, and Leslie K. Anderson
Eating Disorders: Journal of Treatment and Prevention, volume 28, issue 2 (2020), pp. 97–100

Chapter 2

Dialectical behavioral therapy: an update and review of the existing treatment models adapted for adults with eating disorders
Denise Ben-Porath, Florencia Duthu, Tana Luo, Fragiskos Gonidakis, Emilio J. Compte, and Lucene Wisniewski
Eating Disorders: Journal of Treatment and Prevention, volume 28, issue 2 (2020), pp. 101–121

Chapter 3

Dialectical behavioral therapy for the treatment of adolescent eating disorders: a review of existing work and proposed future directions
Erin E. Reilly, Natalia C. Orloff, Tana Luo, Laura A. Berner, Tiffany A. Brown, Kimberly Claudat, Walter H. Kaye, and Leslie K. Anderson
Eating Disorders: Journal of Treatment and Prevention, volume 28, issue 2 (2020), pp. 122–141

Chapter 4

Correlates of co-occurring eating disorders and substance use disorders: a case for dialectical behavior therapy
Kimberly Claudat, Tiffany A. Brown, Leslie Anderson, Gina Bongiorno, Laura A. Berner, Erin Reilly, Tana Luo, Natalia Orloff, and Walter H. Kaye
Eating Disorders: Journal of Treatment and Prevention, volume 28, issue 2 (2020), pp. 142–156

Chapter 5

Self-criticism longitudinally predicts nonsuicidal self-injury in eating disorders
Natalie M. Perkins, Shelby N. Ortiz, and April R. Smith
Eating Disorders: Journal of Treatment and Prevention, volume 28, issue 2 (2020), pp. 157–170

Chapter 6

Outpatient treatment for adults with complex eating disorders and co-morbid conditions: a decision making model and case example
Joanna Marino, Rebecca Hardin, Alexandra Gasbarro, Victoria A Dansereau, and Sarah Fischer
Eating Disorders: Journal of Treatment and Prevention, volume 28, issue 2 (2020), pp. 171–183

Chapter 7

Acceptance-based skill acquisition and cognitive reappraisal in a culturally responsive treatment for binge eating in adolescence
Rebecca C. Kamody, Idia B. Thurston, and E. Thomaseo Burton
Eating Disorders: Journal of Treatment and Prevention, volume 28, issue 2 (2020), pp. 184–201

Chapter 8

Dialectical behavior therapy guided self-help for binge-eating disorder
Therese E. Kenny, Jacqueline C. Carter, and Debra L. Safer
Eating Disorders: Journal of Treatment and Prevention, volume 28, issue 2 (2020), pp. 202–211

Notes on Contributors

Leslie K. Anderson, Eating Disorder Center for Treatment and Research, Department of Psychiatry, University of California, San Diego, California, USA.

Denise Ben-Porath, Department of Psychology, John Carroll University, University Heights, Ohio, USA.

Laura A. Berner, Icahn School of Medicine, Mount Sinai, New York, USA.

Gina Bongiorno, Eating Disorders Center for Treatment and Research, University of California, San Diego, California, USA.

Tiffany A. Brown, Department of Psychological Sciences, Auburn University, Alabama, USA.

E. Thomaseo Burton, Children's Hospital of Philadelphia, Philadelphia, Pennsylvania, USA.

Jacqueline C. Carter, Department of Psychology, Memorial University of Newfoundland, St. John's, Newfoundland, Canada.

Kimberly Claudat, Department of Psychiatry, University of California, San Diego, California, USA.

Emilio J. Compte, Universidad Adolfo Ibáñez, Santiago Metropolitan, Chile; Research Department, Comenzar De Nuevo Treatment Center, Monterrey, México.

Victoria A Dansereau, Spring Grove Hospital Center, Catonsville, Maryland, USA.

Florencia Duthu, DBT-Eating Disorders Team, Fundación Foro, Buenos Aires, Argentina.

Sarah Fischer, Department of Psychology, George Mason University, Fairfax, Virginia, USA.

Alexandra Gasbarro, Montgomery County Counseling Center, Washington, D.C.-Baltimore Area, USA.

Fragiskos Gonidakis, Department of Psychiatry, National and Kapodistrian University of Athens, Athens, Greece.

Rebecca Hardin, Private practice, Potomac Behavioral Solutions, Arlington, Virginia, USA.

Rebecca C. Kamody, Department of Psychiatry, Yale University School of Medicine, New Haven, Connecticut, USA; Department of Psychology, The University of Memphis, Memphis, Tennessee, USA.

Walter H. Kaye, Department of Psychiatry, University of California, San Diego, California, USA.

Therese E. Kenny, Department of Psychology, University of Guelph, Guelph, Ontario, Canada.

Tana Luo, Eating Disorders Center for Treatment and Research, University of California, San Diego, California, USA.

Joanna Marino, Private practice, Potomac Behavioral Solutions, Arlington, Virginia, USA.

Natalia C. Orloff, Department of Psychiatry, University of California, San Diego, California, USA.

Shelby N. Ortiz, School of Medicine, University of North Carolina at Chapel Hill, North Carolina, USA.

Natalie M. Perkins, Department of Psychology, Miami University, Oxford, Ohio, USA.

Erin E. Reilly, Department of Psychiatry, University of California, San Fransisco, California, USA; Department of Psychology, Hofstra University, Hempstead, New York, USA.

Debra L. Safer, Department of Psychiatry and Behavioural Sciences, Stanford University, Stanford, California, USA.

April R. Smith, Department of Psychology, Auburn University, Alabama, USA.

Idia B. Thurston, Institute for Health Equity and Social Justice Research, Northeastern University, Boston, Massachusetts, USA.

Lucene Wisniewski, Center for Evidence Based Treatment, Shaker Heights; Department of Psychological Sciences, Case Western Reserve University, Cleveland, Ohio, USA.

Dialectical behavior therapy for eating disorders: state of the research and new directions

Tiffany A. Brown, Lucene Wisniewski, and Leslie K. Anderson

Overview

Dialectical behavior therapy (DBT) has theoretical and clinical relevance, as well as burgeoning empirical support, for the treatment of eating disorders (ED). Originally developed for patients with Borderline Personality Disorder, DBT works from the perspective that maladaptive, impulsive behaviors function as misguided attempts to regulate unwanted emotions (Linehan, Heard, & Armstrong, 1993). As such, DBT focuses on developing adaptive skillful behaviors to help improve effective self-regulation. Given well-documented associations between difficulties with emotion regulation and eating disorder symptoms (Lavender et al., 2015), a growing body of research has examined the efficacy of DBT for EDs (Bankoff, Karpel, Forbes, & Pantalone, 2012). To date, studies have demonstrated the efficacy of DBT for bulimia nervosa (BN) and binge eating disorder (BED) compared with waitlist (Safer, Telch, & Agras, 2001; Telch, Agras, & Linehan, 2001) and active control conditions (Chen et al., 2017; Safer, Robinson, & Jo, 2010). Per APA practice guidelines, DBT has demonstrated efficacy for the treatment of BED and initial efficacy in the treatment of BN (Yager et al., 2005). Clinically, DBT appears to be a particularly good fit for patients with complex presentations and comorbid disorders; as such, recent research has focused on adapting and applying DBT for these groups (Ben-Porath, Wisniewski, & Warren, 2010; Brown et al., 2018).

Given our clinical and research experience with DBT for individuals with eating disorders, we came together as co-editors of this special issue of Eating Disorders. The Journal of Treatment and Prevention on "Dialectical Behavior Therapy: State of the Research and New Directions." Our goal for this special issue is to summarize the expanding evidence for DBT for eating disorders and comorbid conditions and to illustrate the broad scope of the ongoing work in this important area.

This special issue

We have organized this review into three parts, divided by theme:

Part one: reviews of DBT as applied to adult and adolescent populations

First, Ben-Porath and colleagues (2020) review three major treatment models that have adapted DBT for EDs in adult populations (Stanford Model, Radically Open-DBT, and Multi-diagnostic ED-DBT) and describe the state of the evidence of research for these adaptations of DBT in adult populations. Next, Reilly and colleagues (2020) review research focused specifically on the use of DBT for adolescents with eating disorders, including both those studies applying DBT as the primary treatment and investigations of DBT as an adjunctive treatment.

Part two: complex or comorbid eating disorder presentations and applications for DBT

First, Claudat and colleagues (2020) compare eating disorder patients with and without comorbid substance use disorders (SUD) on comorbid psychopathology, emotion dysregulation, and sensitivity to reward and punishment. Results supported that patients with SUD had a greater number of psychiatric comorbidities, were more sensitive to reward, and had greater difficulty engaging in goal directed activity, higher impulsivity, and more limited access to emotion regulation strategies. The authors discuss the implications of these results for the integrated treatment of eating disorders and SUD using DBT. Next, Perkins, Ortiz, & Smith (2020) present results demonstrating that self-criticism longitudinally predicts non-suicidal self-injury (NSSI) in an eating disorder sample. The authors discuss how treatments like DBT, that target self-criticism and blame, may have promise for directly targeting maintaining mechanisms for NSSI in eating disorders. Finally, Marino and colleagues (2020) describe a clinically-relevant and novel decision-making model for determining when to use DBT rather than cognitive behavior therapy, based on comorbid psychopathology, level of emotion dysregulation, and the presence/absence of NSSI or suicidality. The authors present a case study to help illustrate this model and provide initial descriptive data on patients in an outpatient clinical practice that uses this model.

Part three: adaptations and implementation of DBT

First, Kamody, Thurston, & Burton describe (2020) qualitative data from a culturally-responsive DBT-skills-based intervention for underserved youth with emotional overeating. Participants identified learning acceptance-based DBT skills, particularly radical acceptance, as both highly acceptable and the most useful aspect of treatment. Results show that acceptance-based DBT skills may be associated with change-based cognitive strategies, which may contribute to improvements in reducing emotional overeating in youth. Next, Kenny, Carter-

Major, & Safer (2020) review how DBT for BED has been adapted for self-help delivery, the limited but promising findings available to date, and directions for future research. In particular, the authors emphasize the utility of self-help approaches for DBT in offering a treatment that is less time-consuming and expensive, and has less need for specialized therapist-training, which could allow DBT for BED to be disseminated more easily.

Conclusion

The articles included in this special issue reflect a range of study samples, designs, and methodologies. Further, they provide a sampling of the diverse ways that DBT is being adapted, implemented, and disseminated for patients with eating disorders. We hope that this special issue will, in addition to providing a greater understanding of the current and ongoing research related to DBT for eating disorders, also inspire additional research on DBT for eating disorders. Given how treatment-resistant eating disorders are, and the frequency that they co-occur with other psychiatric diagnoses, we must as a field continue to seek innovative ways to help patients achieve lasting remission. It is hopeful to see the progress that continues to be made towards this goal.

References

Bankoff, S. M., Karpel, M. G., Forbes, H. E., & Pantalone, D. W. (2012). A systematic review of dialectical behavior therapy for the treatment of eating disorders. *Eating Disorders: Journal of Treatment and Prevention, 20*, 196–215. doi:10.1080/10640266.2012.668478

Ben-Porath, D., Duthu, F., Luo, T., Gondakis, F., Compte, E. J., & Wisniewski, L. (2020). Dialectical behavior therapy: An update and review of the existing treatment models adapted for adults with eating disorders. *Eating Disorders, 28*, 2.

Ben-Porath, D. D., Wisniewski, L., & Warren, M. (2010). Outcomes of a day treatment program for eating disorders using clinical and statistical significance. *Journal of Contemporary Psychotherapy, 40*, 115–123. doi:10.1007/s10879-009-9125-5

Brown, T. A., Cusack, A., Anderson, L. K., Trim, J., Nakamura, T., Trunko, M. E., & Kaye, W. H. (2018). Efficacy of a partial hospital programme for adults with eating disorders. *European Eating Disorders Review, 26*, 241–252. doi:10.1002/erv.2589

Chen, E. Y., Cacioppo, J., Fettich, K., Gallop, R., McCloskey, M. S., Olino, T., & Zeffiro, T. A. (2017). An adaptive randomized trial of dialectical behavior therapy and cognitive behavior therapy for binge-eating. *Psychological Medicine, 47*, 703–717. doi:10.1017/S0033291716002543

Claudat, K., Brown, T. A., Anderson, L. K., Bongiorno, G., Berner, L. A., Reilly, E., … Kaye, W. H. (2020). Correlates of Co-occurring eating disorders and substance use disorders: A case for dialectical behavior therapy. *Eating Disorders, 28*, 2.

Kamody, R. C., Thurston, I. B., & Burton, E. T. (2020). Acceptance-based skill acquisition and cognitive reappraisal in a culturally-responsive treatment for binge eating in adolescence. *Eating Disorders, 28*, 2.

Kenny, T. E., Carter-Major, J. C., & Safer, D. L. (2020). Dialectical behavior therapy guided self-help for binge-eating disorder. *Eating Disorders, 28*, 2.

Lavender, J. M., Wonderlich, S. A., Engel, S. G., Gordon, K. H., Kaye, W. H., & Mitchell, J. E. (2015). Dimensions of emotion dysregulation in anorexia nervosa and bulimia nervosa: A conceptual review of the empirical literature. *Clinical Psychology Review, 40*, 111–122. doi:10.1016/j.cpr.2015.05.010

Linehan, M. M., Heard, H. L., & Armstrong, H. E. (1993). Naturalistic follow-up of a behavioral treatment for chronically parasuicidal borderline patients. *Archives of General Psychiatry, 50*, 971–974. doi:10.1001/archpsyc.1993.01820240055007

Marino, J., Hardin, R., Gasbarro, A., Dansereau, V. A., & Fischer, S. (2020). Outpatient treatment for adults with complex eating disorders and co-morbid conditions: A decision making model and case example. *Eating Disorders, 28*, 2.

Perkins, N. M., Ortiz, S. N., & Smith, A. R. (2020). Self-criticism longitudinally predicts nonsuicidal self-injury in eating disorders. *Eating Disorders.* doi:10.1080/10640266.2019.1695450

Reilly, E. E., Orloff, N. C., Luo, T., Berner, L. A., Brown, T. A., Claudat, K., … Anderson, L. K. (2020). Dialectical behavioral therapy for the treatment of adolescent eating disorders: A review of existing work and proposed future directions. *Eating Disorders, 28*, 2.

Safer, D. L., Robinson, A. H., & Jo, B. (2010). Outcome from a randomized controlled trial of group therapy for binge eating disorder: Comparing dialectical behavior therapy adapted for binge eating to an active comparison group therapy. *Behavior Therapy, 41*, 106–120. doi:10.1016/j.beth.2009.01.006

Safer, D. L., Telch, C. F., & Agras, W. S. (2001). Dialectical behavior therapy for bulimia nervosa. *American Journal of Psychiatry, 158*, 632–634. doi:10.1176/appi.ajp.158.4.632

Telch, C. F., Agras, W. S., & Linehan, M. M. (2001). Dialectical behavior therapy for binge eating disorder. *Journal of Consulting and Clinical Psychology, 69*, 1061–1065. doi:10.1037/0022-006X.69.6.1061

Yager, J., Devlin, M. J., Halmi, K. A., Herzog, D. B., Mitchell, J. E., Powers, P. S., & Zerbe, K. J. (2005). Guideline watch: Practice guideline for the treatment of patients with eating disorders. *Focus, 3*, 546–551. doi:10.1176/foc.3.4.546

Dialectical behavioral therapy: an update and review of the existing treatment models adapted for adults with eating disorders

Denise Ben-Porath, Florencia Duthu, Tana Luo, Fragiskos Gonidakis ⓘ, Emilio J. Compte ⓘ, and Lucene Wisniewski

ABSTRACT

Despite the effectiveness of CBT in reducing shape/weight concerns and dietary restraint, research suggests that patients considered recovered may still exhibit emotional difficulties related to eating disorders (EDs). Dialectical behavior therapy (DBT) has been adapted for a variety of mental disorders characterized by emotion dysregulation and, more recently, for EDs specifically. The current review found that the majority of the research studies employed one of the following three adaptations of DBT for EDs: The Stanford Model, Radically Open-DBT (RO-DBT), or Multidiagnostic ED-DBT (MED-DBT). Therefore, this review sought to review and update the empirical research on each adaptation and (2) offer preliminary recommendations for when and which adaptation of DBT to use when treating adults with EDs. Findings from the empirical literature on DBT and EDs indicate that the Stanford Model has the most rigorous and numerous studies demonstrating efficacy and effectiveness in those diagnosed with binge eating disorder. Fewer studies have been conducted using the Stanford Model with bulimia nervosa; therefore, less strong assertions can be made about DBT with those diagnosed with bulimia. The MED-DBT model has been evaluated in several open trials within higher levels of care with promising results, but the lack of randomized clinically-controlled trials prevents a definitive statement about its efficacy. Finally, research on applying the RO-DBT model to anorexia-nervosa, restricting subtype is in its infancy, prohibiting solid conclusions or recommendations regarding its efficacy or effectiveness.

Clinical implications

- Evidence for adaptations for Eating Disorders in adults is presented.
- Findings across research designs and treatment settings are discussed.
- Eating Disorder-Dialectical Behavior Therapy adaptations guidelines suggested.

Dialectical behavior therapy (DBT), was originally developed to treat highly suicidal, self injurious individuals diagnosed with borderline personality disorder (BPD) (Linehan, Armstrong, Suarez, Allmon, & Heard, 1991). Because of the success of DBT in addressing deficits in emotion regulation in those with BPD, it has been applied to comorbidly diagnosed individuals with ED and BPD with promising results (Ben-Porath, Wisniewski, & Warren, 2009; Chen, Matthews, Allen, Kuo, & Linehan, 2008; Kröger et al., 2010; Palmer et al., 2003). In fact, some theorists have argued that ED symptoms represent a maladaptive method to regulate negative affect (Heatherton & Baumeister, 1991; Safer, Telch, & Agras, 2001; Safer, Telch, & Chen, 2009; Telch, Agras, & Linehan, 2000, 2001), and several studies have demonstrated that negative mood states are reduced in women after a binge eating episode (Polivy & Herman, 1993).

Thus, some have suggested that eating disorder (ED) patients present with issues related to emotional undercontrol, such as those diagnosed with binge eating disorder (BED) and bulimia nervosa (BN) who use bingeing and/or purging to regulate emotions (Telch et al., 2000), while other researchers have posited that some ED patients present with emotional overcontrol, such as those diagnosed with anorexia nervosa (AN), who may restrict food to regulate affect (Hempel, Vanderbleek, & Lynch, 2018). While symptom presentation may vary amongst ED subtypes, difficulties in affect regulation appear to be a core problem for all who struggle with EDs, and, as such, there has been a growing interest in applying DBT to individuals diagnosed with EDs.

Bankoff, Karpel, Forbes, and Pantalone (2012) conducted the first systematic review of the empirical literature on DBT for EDs. Their review consisted of 13 peer- reviewed articles published between the years of 2000 to 2011. Collectively the reviewed studies indicated that DBT is effective in reducing ED behaviors. While fewer studies in the review examined abstinence rates (defined as refraining from binging or purging for one month), those that did found encouraging findings, with rates ranging from 29% to 89% at post treatment. Data examining individuals diagnosed with comorbid BPD and ED found similar results, with the studies demonstrating a reduction in ED symptoms and remission rates ranging from 33% to 50%. Findings were equivocal with respect to improvement in mood symptoms and social functioning, suggesting that the role of affect regulation in maintaining ED symptoms is less well understood. In a meta-analysis of randomized controlled trials of third-wave behavioral therapies, including DBT, Linardon, Fairburn, Fitzsimmons-Craft, Wilfley, and Brennan (2017) concluded that DBT was "possibly efficacious" for the treatment of BN and BED. With slightly broader inclusion criteria, Lenz, Taylor, Fleming, and Serman (2014) evaluated nine studies utilizing between and within-subjects designs. Both between subjects design studies ($n = 4$) and within-subjects design studies ($n = 4$) indicated a large effect size with respect to eating disorder symptoms and a medium effect size with respect to depression symptoms. Likely a result of the small sample size ($n = 8$), the one remaining study (Chen et al., 2008) of the nine yielded a small effect size on eating disorder symptoms.

In sum, the research for DBT in those with EDs is still in its nascent stages as no study has yet to conduct a randomized trial comparing DBT to an established treatment for EDs such as cognitive behavioral therapy (CBT) or interpersonal therapy (IPT). Despite this, the data reviewed do seem to indicate that DBT is superior to no treatment, is likely efficacious in treating some ED diagnoses, and may improve psychosocial functioning and mood symptoms in some patients.

Interpretation of these findings and the application of DBT to EDs is complex, in part because the majority of the studies published have utilized adaptations of DBT for EDs. For example, in the Bankoff et al. (2012) review, 12 of the 13 studies reviewed employed an adaptation of DBT for EDs, which included either the Stanford Model for outpatient BED and BN (DBT-BED;DBT-BN) or DBT adapted for EDs treated in higher levels of care called the Multidiagnostic Complex Eating Disorders for DBT Model (MED-DBT; Federici, Wisniewski, & Ben-Porath, 2012). Since the Bankoff et al. (2012) review, an additional model, Radically Open-DBT (RO-DBT), has been developed for those diagnosed with anorexia nervosa, restricting subtype (AN-R; Lynch et al., 2013).

Thus, a primary aim of the current review is to provide an update to the Bankoff et al. (2012) review of the literature on DBT and EDs. In an effort to do this, we searched the electronic database, PsycInfo, using the same terms (e.g., *DBT or dialectical behavior therapy and eating disorder anorexia, bulimia, or binge eating)* that were used in the Bankoff et al. (2012) review. This resulted in 232 articles. We further narrowed the search by limiting articles from August 2011 (where the Bankoff et al. review ended) until the present (December 2019). This search resulted in 138 articles. From these abstracts, like Bankoff et al. (2012), we selected for inclusion, English-language, peer-reviewed, journals with empirical data for which the target population was adults diagnosed with EDs. This left 19 remaining studies. From these, 6 studies were excluded due to the lack of treatment outcome data ($n = 3$), confounding treatment interventions intermingled with DBT ($n = 2$), or limited information about the treatment ($n = 1$). This left 13 studies. By searching the reference section from selected articles, four additional studies were found (Brown et al., 2018, 2019a; 2019b; Carter, Kennedy, Singleton, Van Wijk, & Heath, 2019) bringing the count up to 17. Similar to Bankoff et al. (2012), with the exception of two studies (Courbasson, Nishikawa, & Dixon, 2012; Navarro-Haro et al., 2018), all of the remaining 15 articles reviewed used one of the following adaptations of DBT for EDs: (1) The Stanford Model, (2) RO-DBT, or (3) DBT-MED.

While these adaptations of DBT to EDs may be necessary to effectively treat ED symptoms, scientist-practitioners may not know which model to use, under which circumstances, and for which patients. Therefore, the goal of this review is to provide a brief overview of each of these three adaptations and then summarize the empirical research on each since the Bankoff et al. (2012) review (see Table 1). Given that the studies prior to August 2011 have already been described in greater depth, they will not be reviewed in detail. (Interested readers are referred to Bankoff et al., 2012 for a more thorough review of these previous studies.) A final aim of this review is to offer preliminary recommendations based upon the current literature for when and which adaptation of DBT to use when treating adults with EDs.

The stanford model: DBT-BED and DBT-BN

The first and most widely researched DBT adaptation for EDs is what has been referred to as the Stanford Model for BED and BN or DBT-BED/DBT-BN. Although CBT has been the treatment of choice for decades with respect to BN and BED, as many as half the patients treated with CBT do not respond (Haye, Bacaltchuk, & Stefano, 2009). Several studies indicate that individuals diagnosed with BED and BN often report engaging in ED behaviors when emotionally dysregulated (Arnow, Kenardy, & Agras, 1992). Thus, this adaptation, which proposes that bingeing and/or purging occur as a way to regulate painful affect, was developed to address emotion regulation deficits found in those with BN and BED (Linehan & Chen, 2005; Waller, 2003; Wiser & Telch, 1999; Wisniewski & Kelly, 2003).

Review of the empirical literature on DBT- BED and DBT-BN

Several uncontrolled clinical trials (Chen et al., 2008; Safer, Lively, Telch, & Agras, 2002; Safer, Telch, Agras, 2001) and randomized clinical trials (RCT; Safer, Robinson, & Jo, 2010; Safer et al., 2001; Telch et al., 2001) have been conducted using DBT-BED/BN for adults with EDs. These studies have yielded promising results, including abstinence from binge eating at rates ranging from 64% to 89% (Safer et al., 2010; Telch et al., 2001), improvements in weight, shape, and eating concerns (Telch et al., 2001), and quicker response rates in those assigned to DBT-BED as compared to active comparison group treatment (ACGT; Safer et al., 2010).

Since the Bankoff et al. (2012) review, five RCTs (Carter, Kennedy, Singleton, Van Wijk, & Heath, 2019; Chen et al., 2017; Masson, von Ranson, Wallace, & Safer, 2013; Rahmani, Omidi, Asemi, & Akbari, 2018; Robinson & Safer, 2012), and three uncontrolled clinical trials (Erb, Farmer, & Mehlenbeck, 2013; Klein, Skinner, & Hawley, 2012; Mushquash & McMahan, 2015) using DBT with BED or BN have been conducted. Of these nine studies, eight employed the Stanford Model for DBT-BED/BN.

Like studies reviewed in Bankoff et al. (2012), findings continue to demonstrate that DBT is efficacious for those diagnosed with BED. Utilizing DBT-BED,

Table 1. Overview of Studies Examining DBT/BED, MED-DBT, and RO-DBT for ED in Adults since 2011.

Study	Design	Sample Size	Sample Demographics	Treatment/ Setting	Outcomes	Follow up	Results
DBT/BED							
Robinson and Safer (2012)	RCT	101	Mage: 52.2 years; 85% female; 100% BED; 76% Caucasian, 13% Latino, 5% Asian, 3% African American.	20 weekly (2h) DBT/BED-group sessions Vs. Active comparison group therapy (ACGT).	Putative moderators (demographic variables, ED & general psychopathology).		Participants with Avoidant Personality Disorder or an earlier onset of overweight/ dieting evidenced significantly worsened outcome when treated with ACGT versus DBT/ BED.
Klein et al. (2012)	UCT	5	*Mage*: 39.6 years; 100% female; 100% with either sub-threshold and full-threshold BED or BN; 100% Caucasian.	16-weeks (2-2½h) DBT/BED-group sessions.	Binge eating and attrition.	-	Large reductions in the primary outcome of weekly binge frequency from pretreatment to post-treatment. Attrition was elevated compared with previous efficacy trials.
Erb et al. (2013)	Case Report	3	*Mage*: 44.3 years; 100% female; 100% BED; 33.3% Asian, 33% Caucasian, 33% Hispanic	12-weekly sessions (1 online) of DBT/BED-based (2h) skills-training group, and addition interpersonal skills.	Binge eating frequency and eating psychopathology.	12 months	Participants demonstrated clinically significant reduction in disordered eating behavior and improvements in self-esteem, emotion regulation, and quality of life. Treatment gains were maintained at follow-up.
Masson et al. (2013)	Pilot RCT	60	*Mage*: 42.8 years; 88.3% female; 100% BED; 90%-93.1% Caucasian.	DBT guided self-help (DBTgsh) (orientation session, manual, and six 20-min support calls over 13 weeks) Vs. Waiting list.	Binge eating episodes and abstinence from binge eating.	6 months	DBTgsh participants reported significantly fewer binge eating episodes and greater rates of abstinence from binge eating than controls. At 6-month follow-up, DBTgsh participants had improved quality of life and reduced eating psychopathology compared to baseline.

(*Continued*)

Table 1. (Continued).

Study	Design	Sample Size	Sample Demographics	Treatment/ Setting	Outcomes	Follow up	Results
Mushquash and McMahan (2015)	UCT	11	*Mage*: 44.6 years; 90.9% female; 100% patients seeking bariatric services; 81.8% Caucasian.	10 weekly (2h) DBT/BED-group sessions.	Binge eating severity and eating psychopathology.	-	On average participants showed a significant reduction in binge eating severity from baseline to post-treatment, but not for the remaining variables on eating psychopathology. Low dropout rates suggest that DBT/BED is acceptable to patients.
Chen et al. (2017)	RCT	109	*Mage*: 38.2 years; 100% female; 73.4% Caucasian; 71.6% BED;28.4% BN .	Participants received a guided self-help CBT (cGSH) manual + 4 sessions (30/min). After session 4, strong responders continued in the cGSH. Weak responders were randomized to either 6 months of DBT or an adapted CBT treatment (CBT+).	Binge eating frequency and attrition	6 & 12 months	Regardless of assigned treatment, all participants no longer met criteria for BED/BN at the end of treatment. However, early strong responders treated with cGSH had faster and greater reductions in binge episodes as compared to those in the DBT or the CBT+ conditions. At a six and then 12-month follow-up gains were maintained in all treatment conditions with no significant differences among groups in binge episodes. No differences were observed in treatment attrition across treatment groups
Rahmani et al. (2018)	RCT	60	*Mage*: 29.8–31.3 years; 100% female; 100% Overweight-BED.	20 DBT/BED-group sessions (2h) twice a week Vs. Waiting list.	Binge eating, weight and emotional regulation	-	DBT/BED improved BMI, binge eating and emotion regulation ability.

(Continued)

Table 1. (Continued).

Study	Design	Sample Size	Sample Demographics	Treatment/ Setting	Outcomes	Follow up	Results
Carter, Kenny, Singleton, Van Wijk, & Heath (2019)	RCT	71	*M*age: 40.2–41 years; 91.7%-95.7% female; 100% BED; 91.7%-95.7% Caucasian, other 4.3%-8.3%.	12-week DBT guided self-help (DBT-GSH) (30-min/2-week initial, 3 biweekly, and final guided sessions), vs. 12-week active control condition (self-esteem and DBT unguided self help (SE-USH, DBT-USH).	Binge eating, ED psychopathology, general psychological distress, and health-related quality of life.	3 months	There was a significant decrease in binge frequency from pre- to post-treatment that did not differ across groups, which it was maintained at follow-up in all three conditions. The pattern of results for the other outcome measures was also a significant improvement in all three conditions that was maintained at follow-up, with no statistically significant across groups.
RO-DBT							
Lynch et al. (2013)	UCT	47	*M*age: 27.1 years; 100% female; 100% AN; 94.1% Caucasian.	Inpatient Radically Open-DBT (RO-DBT) program (22 weeks average)	Weight, eating psychopathology and quality of life	-	RO-DBT was associated with significant improvements in weight gain, reductions in ED psychopathology and increases in ED-related quality of life.
Chen et al. (2015).	Case Series	6 & 9	*M*age: 32.3–27.6 years; 100% female; 100% AN or subclinical AN; 80% Caucasian.	Case Series 1: standard DBT; Case series 2: DBT augmented with skills addressing over-control.	BMI, eating psychopathology.	6 & 12 months	Case Series 1 and 2 resulted in an increase in BMI and an improvement in eating psychopathology, with larger effect sizes for Case Series 2. Adding skills addressing over controlled emotions and behaviors may be helpful.

(*Continued*)

Table 1. (Continued).

Study	Design	Sample Size	Sample Demographics	Treatment/ Setting	Outcomes	Follow up	Results
MED-DBT							
Federici and Wisniewski (2013)	Case Series	7	*Mage*: 23.9 years; 100% female; 100% Multi-diagnostic ED Presentations; 100% Caucasian.	6-month Multi-diagnostic ED-DBT Outpatient Program (6h/ day, 5 days/week) or intensive programming (3h/day, 3–5 days/ week).	ED symptoms, self-harm, weight, medical stability, hospitalizations over the course of treatment, client and clinician program acceptability.	-	Treatment was associated with reductions in ED symptoms, suicidal and self-injurious behaviors, treatment interfering behaviors, psychiatric and medical hospitalizations, and clinician burnout.
Ben-Porath et al. (2014)	UCT	65	*Mage*: 23.4 years; 100% female; 4.6% AN, 29.2% AN with regular menses, 66.2% BN.	5-days per week (6h) CBT-ED based treatment program, and weekly DBT skills-training group (2h). Median length: 20 days.	Affect regulation, eating psychopathology.	-	Participants demonstrated a significant improvement in their ability to regulate affect. Also, participants showed a significant increase in weight gain, reduction in restriction, bingeing, purging and eating disordered cognitions.
Brown et al. (2018)	ND	243	*Mage*: 26.6 years; 94.7% female; 51.4% AN spectrum, 48.6% BN spectrum; 74.7% Caucasian, 5.4% Asian, 1.2% African American, 0.4% Native American/Alaskan, 18.3% other (21% identified as Latino).	PHP (up to 6 days/week, 6-10h/ day). Full DBT (2h/week skills-group, individual therapy, team consultation, phone coaching) + variety of evidence-based groups (applied DBT, RO-DBT, CBT, CBT-E). Patients went into IOP before discharge. Mean length 89.2 days.	ED behaviors and psychopathology, BMI, depressive symptoms, and trait anxiety.	3, 6, 12 & 24 months	Results support the efficacy of PHP across all primary outcomes variables (BMI, binge/ purge frequency, and ED psychopathology) from intake to discharge and across follow-up for AN-R and BN patients. All diagnoses demonstrated significant improvements at discharge on depression and anxiety measures, and patients maintained these improvements at follow-up

(*Continued*)

Table 1. (Continued).

Study	Design	Sample Size	Sample Demographics	Treatment/ Setting	Outcomes	Follow up	Results
Brown et al. (2019a)	ND	135	*M*age: 25.1 years, 93.3% female; 29.6% ANR, 11.9% ANBP, 42.9% BN, 3% BED, 12.6% OSFED; (70.4% mood, 68.9% anxiety, 3.7% alcohol use, & 4.4% SUD); 72.6% Caucasian, 9.6% Asian, 1.5% African American, 16.2% other (17.6% Hispanic).	DBT-based PHP program focused on weight restoration (10h/day, 6-day/week). Patient went into IOP before discharge to regular outpatient care. Mean length 97.1 days.	ED psychopathology, depression symptoms, emotion dysregulation symptoms.	-	DBT skills use predicted greater improvements in ED, depressive, and emotion dysregulation symptoms from treatment admission to discharge. Notably, early versus later change in skills use was a stronger predictor of outcome.
Brown et al. (2019b)	ND		*M*age: 26.63 years; 95% female; 32% ANR, 19% ANBP, 49% BN (78.4% mood, 75.5% anxiety, 7.5% alcohol use, & 8.7% SUD); 74.9% Caucasian, 5.0% Asian, 1.3% African American, 0.4% Native American, other (18.4%).	DBT-based PHP program focused on weight restoration (10h/day, 6-day/week). Patients step down to IOP before discharge to regular outpatient care. Mean length 88.7 days	Emotion regulation and ED symptomology	*M*days until follow up assessment post discharge: 309.58	BN patients demonstrated improvements in emotion regulation from pre to post treatment and at follow-up. ANBP and ANR patients demonstrated improvement in emotion regulation from admission to discharge, but did not maintain improvement at follow-up; Changes in emotion regulation were moderately associated with improvement in ED pathology at discharge but not at follow up.

ND = naturalistic design; RCT = randomized control trial; UCT = uncontrolled trial; CBT = cognitive behavioral therapy; CBT-E = Cognitive Behavioral Therapy-Enhanced; DBT = dialectical behavioral therapy; IOP = intensive outpatient treatment; PHP = partial hospital programs; ED = eating disorder; AN = anorexia nervosa; ANBP = anorexia nervosa binge/purge subtype; ANR = anorexia nervosa restrictive subtype; BN = bulimia nervosa; BED = binge eating disorders; EDNOS = eating disorders not otherwise specified; OSFED = other specified feeding or eating disorder; BPD = borderline personality disorder; MDD = major depressive disorder, PTSD = post-traumatic stress disorder; SUD = substance use disorder.

Rahmani et al. (2018) investigated the efficacy of DBT by randomly assigning 60 individuals diagnosed with BED to either 20 two-hour DBT group sessions twice a week or to a wait-list control condition. Individuals in the DBT arm of the study reported significant reductions in binge eating episodes, lower BMIs, greater improvements in emotion regulation, and better treatment retention as compared to those in the wait-list condition.

Given the growing body of research on the efficacy of DBT-BED, researchers have begun to explore more complex research questions in this population such as identifying treatment outcome moderators and differential treatment response rates to DBT-BED. Toward this end, Robinson and Safer (2012) sought to explore treatment moderators in a randomized controlled trial in 101 adults diagnosed with BED. Participants were randomly assigned to 20 group-DBT sessions or an ACGT. Results indicated that participants with avoidant personality disorder or an earlier onset of dieting/weight issues evidenced significantly worse outcomes when treated with ACGT vs. DBT-BED.

Investigating the differential treatment effects of DBT and CBT-enhanced in early-weak responders, Chen et al. (2017) provided four weeks of CBT-guided self-help (CBTgsh) to women diagnosed with BED or BN. Early-strong responders continued on in CBTgsh for the remainder of the study. Those who were identified as early-weak responders (e.g., no appreciable improvement after 4 sessions of GSH) were randomly assigned to either DBT or CBT-enhanced. Results indicated that early-strong responders who received CBTgsh had somewhat quicker and greater reductions in objective binge days compared to those who were randomized to DBT or CBT-enhanced, but these differences were small. At the end of treatment, early-weak responders in both DBT and CBT-enhanced exhibited reductions in objective binge days, but these improvements were smaller than those found in early-strong responders who received CBTgsh. While CBTgsh overall was superior to DBT and CBT-enhanced, these findings may have been due to selection bias in the CBTgsh group.

Given the success of DBT-BED, many have begun to explore translational research with DBT-BED by implementing self-help interventions guided by the Stanford Model. For example, Masson et al. (2013) tested the effectiveness of a 13-week DBT-guided self-help (DBTgsh) protocol in women diagnosed with BED. The DBTgsh protocol included one in-person, 45-minute orientation session to the DBT skills manual, as well as six supportive phone calls over the course of treatment. Participants in the study were randomly assigned to DBTgsh vs a wait list condition. Results indicated fewer binge eating episodes and greater abstinence rates in the DBTgsh group compared to the control condition at post-treatment and at a 6-month follow-up.

Following up on this research, Carter, Kennedy, Singleton, Van Wijk, and Heath (2019) randomly assigned 71 participants who met criteria for BED to one of three conditions: (1) DBT-unguided self-help (DBT-USH), where participants received a copy of *DBT Solution for Emotional Eating* (Safer, Adler, & Masson, 2018) to review, (2) DBT-guided self-help (DBT-GSH), where participants received a copy of *DBT Solution for Emotional Eating* to review and attended six 30-minute web-based sessions, or (3) Self-esteem-unguided self-help (SE-USH), where participants received a copy of *Self-esteem: A Proven Program of Cognitive Techniques for Assessing, Improving, and Maintaining Your Self-esteem* (McKay & Fanning, 2016) to review. After 12 weeks, all participants regardless of condition reported a decrease in binge eating. Compared to the other two conditions, the DBT-GSH group demonstrated the greatest reduction in binge frequency and had the fewest people engaging in binge eating at diagnostic levels at post treatment. Despite these promising findings, none of the groups differed significantly. This may have been due to the high attrition across all treatment groups leaving the study significantly underpowered.

While not as methodologically stringent as randomized trials, several uncontrolled clinical trials and case studies have been conducted using DBT-BED since the Bankoff et al. (2012) review. For example, Klein et al. (2012) examined the Stanford adaptations for BED and BN in individuals diagnosed with sub- or full-threshold BED or BN. After 16 weeks of 2-½ hour group DBT sessions (plus phone coaching), participants demonstrated significant reductions in binge eating and improvement in secondary cognitive outcomes related to ED behaviors. While not diagnosed with BED, 11 individuals undergoing pre-treatment interventions for bariatric surgery participated in 10-weekly, 2-hour group DBT-BED sessions. Findings indicated significant improvements in binge eating from pre- to post-intervention, but not in psychosocial functioning (Mushquash & McMahan, 2015). Finally, participants from one small case study on DBT for BED demonstrated reductions in binge eating frequency as well as failure to meet criteria for BED at the end of treatment (Erb et al., 2013).

Taken in total these studies indicate strong evidence for the use of DBT for those diagnosed with BED. Several well controlled RCTs have demonstrated its efficacy with this population. Less well-researched, however, is DBT-BN. The studies that have utilized DBT for this population have also included individuals diagnosed with BED, which may artificially inflate the outcomes given the known success of DBT for BED and the better prognosis for those with BED compared to BN. A needed next step is RCTs in samples that are exclusively diagnosed with BN to parse out differential response to DBT treatment in these two groups.

Radically open-DBT for eating disorders (RO-DBT) model

While the DBT-BED/BN adaptation and standard DBT focus on addressing deficits related to emotion dysregulation, individuals diagnosed with AN-R often present as emotionally overcontrolled. Indeed, existing research indicates that anorexia is associated with low novelty-seeking (Rossier, Bolognini, Plancherel, & Halfon, 2000), heightened threat sensitivity (Harrison, Sullivan, Tchanturia, & Treasure, 2010), low sensitivity to reward (Harrison, O'Brien, Lopez, & Treasure, 2010), cognitive rigidity (Tchanturia et al., 2012), inhibited emotional expression/recognition (Geller, Cockell, Hewitt, Goldner, and Flett (2000), and loneliness (Zucker et al., 2007).

RO-DBT theorizes that, over time, temperamental threat sensitivity interacts with feedback from the environment that emphasizes self-control and minimizing mistakes, which results in impairment in individuals' ability to feel safe (Hempel et al., 2018). Thus, RO-DBT presents a unique conceptualization of restrictive eating behaviors as a maladaptive inhibitory control behavior that allows individuals with AN-R to dampen these negative emotions. While this specific theory of overcontrol as it applies to restrictive ED behaviors has yet to be empirically tested, the four modules in DBT have each been adapted to teach skills that address problematic behaviors that are driven by overcontrol. In addition, a new skills module, radical openness is considered the core skill set of RO-DBT, and is based on three features: openness, flexibility, and connectedness. Thus, rather than focusing on weight restoration, RO-DBT teaches individuals skills that target the issues of overcontrol that are thought to underlie problematic behaviors, emotions, and cognitions, (Lynch et al., 2013).

Review of the empirical literature on RO-DBT

At the time of the Bankoff et al. (2012) review, no empirical studies had been published on RO-DBT. Since this time, two studies have been published with promising outcomes. Lynch et al. (2013) in an open, uncontrolled clinical trial treated 47 inpatients diagnosed with AN-R with RO-DBT with an average length of treatment of 21.7 weeks. The response rate was high with 35% in full remission and 55% in partial remission at discharge. Treatment completers also demonstrated significant improvements in eating disorder symptoms and quality of life, as well as reductions in psychological distress. Interestingly, 72% who completed the inpatient treatment program demonstrated substantial gains in BMI despite weight gain not being actively targeted in this treatment. Thus, this increase in BMI may be due to the inherent structure present in inpatient settings, including set meal times.

Chen et al. (2015) reported results from two case series of DBT for adult AN outpatients. The first group (n = 6) of AN or subclinical AN patients was treated with standard DBT and the DBT for binge eating manual from 4 to 24 months, with one patient dropping out. At the end of the treatment, the improvement in BMI yielded a medium effect size. The second group ($n = 9$) consisted primarily of EDNOS patients with AN symptoms. This group was treated with standard DBT augmented with a skills module for over controlled emotions and behaviors. Treatment ranged from 4 to 12 months, with one dropout. Pre- to post-treatment improvement in BMI yielded a large effect size that was maintained at both 6- and 12-month follow-ups (Chen et al., 2015). The results of these two case series showed a similar effect size of DBT for AN to other treatments specific for outpatient AN.

Adding a skills training module targeting rigidity and increasing openness and social connectedness could possibly increase the effectiveness of DBT for AN, particularly for those with AN-R. However, no RCTs have yet been conducted using RO-DBT. Given the absence of a wait-list condition or comparison group in the two existing studies of RO-DBT for EDs, it is impossible to conclude whether these symptomatic improvements are due to time, maturation, non-specific effects inherent in general inpatient/outpatient treatment, or the actual intervention of RO-DBT. Thus, these initial findings, while promising for targeting overcontrolled symptoms in restricting-type eating disorders, should be interpreted with cautious optimism.

Multidiagnostic complex EDs (MED-DBT) model for higher levels of care

MED-DBT was developed to address multi-diagnostic, highly complex individuals diagnosed with an ED who may require a higher level of ED care (e.g., 9–30 hours of treatment per week) due to the severity of ED symptoms and/or comorbid diagnoses, including, but not limited to, BPD (see Federici et al., 2012 for a more detailed discussion of the treatment development). Indeed, Johnson, Tobin, and Dennis (1990) have speculated that the one-third of patients who typically do not respond to traditional treatments are likely ED individuals who are also comorbidly diagnosed with BPD. While several studies have found promising results using standard DBT in individuals with BPD and EDs, these studies recruited individuals to DBT settings that specialized in BPD and for which the BPD diagnosis was considered primary and the ED diagnosis secondary (Chen et al., 2008; Navarro-Haro et al., 2018; Palmer et al., 2003).

Patients in an ED higher level of care are admitted because the ED diagnosis is primary and yet these patients may also present with multiple comorbid diagnoses, such as BPD. The increased level of severity of the ED symptoms combined with comorbid diagnoses pose significant therapeutic challenges for clinicians as these patients frequently fail numerous outpatient treatments, engage in significant TIBs, present with self-harm and suicidality, and exhibit ED symptoms severe enough to be life-threatening. An added complexity of these presentations is the potential for additional diagnoses and/or BPD to thwart the progress of ED treatment or worse, elevate the ED to a life-threatening crisis.

Thus, MED-DBT combines evidence-based CBT for EDs (Fairburn, 2008) with the empirically supported treatment of DBT for managing multiple high-risk behaviors (e.g., suicidality, NSSI, exercising while having cardiac complications due to the eating disorder, etc.) in the context of significant TIBs and emotion dysregulation. The MED-DBT program emphasizes patient responsibility and flexibility in defining and achieving their treatment goals, while the therapist creates a therapeutic environment that is collaborative, yet grounded in behavioral principles, including contingency management to assist the patient in reaching those goals (Wisniewski & Ben-Porath, 2015).

Review of the empirical literature on the MED-DBT model

Prior to 2012, the research on using DBT to treat individuals with multi-diagnostic and complex EDs was limited. Neither the treatment provided nor the environment within which it was offered could be considered uniform. Specifically, some studies offered standard DBT to complex/comorbid ED patients in an outpatient, weekly format (Chen et al., 2008) or standard DBT with an added skills module directed at EDs (Palmer et al., 2003). Other studies provided DBT within a partial hospitalization program (Ben-Porath et al., 2009) or within an adapted inpatient DBT program (Kröger et al., 2010).

The majority of the studies (5/7) since the Bankoff et al. (2012) review have utilized the DBT-MED model in a higher level of care. The two notable exceptions are Courbasson et al. (2012) and Navarro-Haro et al. (2018), both of which used a non-randomized treatment design comparing DBT to treatment as usual (TAU) in an outpatient setting. Courbasson et al. (2012), for example, compared outpatient DBT to treatment as usual (TAU) in individuals comorbidly diagnosed with ED and substance use disorder (SUD). Individuals in the DBT condition showed significant improvement in affect regulation and a decrease in emotional eating as well an increase in the ability to resist urges to use substances. Indeed, those in the TAU condition did so poorly (e.g., high drop-out rates, worsening of symptoms), recruitment in the TAU condition was terminated prematurely. Navarro-Haro et al. (2018) compared DBT to TAU-CBT for those comorbidly diagnosed with ED and BPD in an outpatient setting. Although those in the DBT condition showed a greater decrease in non-suicidal self-injurious behaviors and depressive symptoms, similar improvements between groups were seen in suicide attempts, ED symptoms, and hospitalizations. While those patients in the TAU-CBT condition fared considerably better than those in the Courbasson et al. (2012) study, these differences may have been due to the more robust TAU condition in the Navarro-Haro et al. (2018) study in which patients received TAU-CBT rather than components of CBT, motivational interviewing, and relapse prevention strategies provided in the Courbasson et al. (2012) study.

The remaining five studies, since the Bankoff et al. (2012) review have investigated the effectiveness of DBT-MED with severe and complex ED patients in a higher level of care. Federici and Wisniewski (2013) treated seven ED patients utilizing the MED-DBT in a day treatment program, all of whom presented with comorbid BPD, additional Axis I diagnoses, and extensive histories of ED treatment failure. Treatment completion for all seven women was associated with reductions in ED symptoms, suicidal and self-injurious behaviors, therapy-interfering behaviors, psychiatric and medical hospitalizations, and clinician burnout.

Extending these findings, by exploring not only ED symptoms but also the impact of DBT on affect regulation, Ben-Porath, Federici, Wisniewski, and Warren (2014) employed the MED-DBT adaptation to 65 patients admitted to a day hospital treatment program. Results indicated a significant increase in weight gain, a significant reduction in ED behaviors (e.g., restriction, bingeing and purging) and a reduction in ED cognitions. Notably, findings indicated an improvement in participants' ability to regulate affect, suggesting that DBT treatment may play an important role in producing changes in affect regulation (Ben-Porath et al., 2014).

In a more recent study evaluating treatment in a day hospital program, Brown et al. (2018) studied the impact of MED-DBT on 241 patients with long standing EDs and significant comorbidity. Results of this open trial demonstrated a significant improvement in weight and comorbidity and ED symptoms, with 49% of patients meeting criteria for full or partial remission at discharge and 37% at one-year follow-up.

Extending these findings, Brown et al. (2019a), utilizing the MED-DBT hierarchy for complex and severe EDs, examined the impact of early vs. later skill acquisition on ED outcomes in a partial hospitalization setting. Given that previous research has established the importance of DBT skills in improvements in those with BPD, these authors hypothesized that the acquisition of DBT skills in ED patients with early change in DBT skills use (e.g., change in skill use from treatment admission to first month) would demonstrate greater improvements in ED symptoms, mood, and emotion regulation as compared to individuals who had later change in DBT skills use (e.g., change in skill use from first month to discharge). While participants improved on all measures from admission to discharge, those with early change in DBT skills use accounted for a larger proportion of the variance in depressive symptoms, emotion dysregulation, and in particular, ED symptoms, indicating the importance of assessing for early skill use and acquisition.

Finally, Brown et al. (2019b) examined improvements in emotion regulation in 241 individuals receiving ED treatment in a day hospital setting. Results indicated improvement in affect regulation, as measured by the DERS score, from admission to discharge in all ED diagnostic groups, including AN-R, AN-BP, and BN. However, only those individuals diagnosed with BN maintained those improvements at follow-up. Of those diagnosed with AN-R, AN-BP, and BN, 24%, 36%, and 26.2% respectively made significant and reliable change at post-treatment. RCI indices were comparable from admission to follow-up for all groups with the exception of the BN sample in which 42.1% at follow up had achieved reliable and significant change on the DERS-total score.

In summary, the MED-DBT model shows promise in impacting ED pathology as well as emotion regulation when offered in the context of partial hospital or inpatient programs. However, firm conclusions and recommendations about its use cannot be made in the absence of more rigorous studies that employ a control group.

Conclusions and recommendations

The studies on DBT adapted for EDs have generally produced positive outcomes, although the research has varied considerably with respect to the amount and rigor. For example, the Stanford Model has the most rigorous and numerous studies demonstrating efficacy but mostly in those diagnosed with BED. Considerably fewer studies have been conducted using the Stanford Model with BN; therefore, less strong assertions can be made about DBT with those diagnosed with BN. The MED-DBT model has been evaluated in several open trials within higher levels of care with promising results, but the lack of RCTs prevents a definitive statement about its efficacy. Finally, research on applying the RO-DBT model to AN-R is in its infancy, prohibiting solid conclusions or recommendations regarding its efficacy or effectiveness.

In the meantime, clinicians are in need of guidance. Clinicians who treat EDs are interested in the potential utility of a DBT model for those ED patients who are not helped by other evidence-based approaches. Additionally, clinicians who are trained in DBT are curious about how they might use their expertise to address eating disorder thoughts and behaviors. Lack of research data does not always dissuade clinicians from adopting approaches, and this may be especially true for individuals who do not respond to standard treatments, as there are even fewer guidelines and data to inform clinical practice with ED patients that fail treatment.

In addition to reviewing the literature and describing the various DBT models for EDs, the ultimate goal of this paper was to provide recommendations regarding which model to use with adult ED patients. As referenced in Table 2, when attempting to make a decision about the use of DBT with an adult ED patient, the clinician must ask several questions: (1) What is the primary ED diagnosis? (2) Has an adequate trial of an EBT for that ED diagnosis been tried? (3) Why might DBT be indicated, and finally, (4) Which DBT model is indicated? Although not directly addressed in this paper, it is also strongly recommended that the clinician

Table 2. Summary of when to consider using DBT to treat adult EDs.

ED Diagnosis	Front line evidence-based treatment	When to consider DBT	Type of DBT to consider	Comments
AN-R	No approach identified as superior	When more well studied treatments have not been effective or when emotional overcontrol is hindering treatment effectiveness	RO-DBT	An alternative to more well-studied treatments. Does not address eating directly. Must have physician on team to ensure medical stability.
BED	CBT-ED	When CBT-ED has not been effective or when emotional regulation is hindering treatment effectiveness	Stanford	An alternative to CBT. Well studied and effective.
BN	CBT-ED	When CBT-ED has not been effective or when emotional regulation is hindering treatment effectiveness	Stanford	More research needed on the use of this model with BN specifically.
Complex/ Multi-diagnostic ED	CBT-ED	At least 2 of the following -CBT-ED has not been effective - comorbid diagnoses - significant emotion dysregulation -. ED life threatening - history of TIB	MED-DBT	Standard DBT enhanced with strategies for ED symptomatology and alteration in DBT targeting to adjust for the ED symptoms. Mostly studied in IOP and DTP. Preliminary results show effectiveness. Requires well designed RCT.

ask: "Do I have the skills to adequately address these problems or do I need more training in order to provide this treatment effectively?" The recommendations below are meant to act as a guideline, as well as a catalyst for clinicians to determine areas of competence and areas where more research and/or training is needed.

If the patient has an uncomplicated BED, and has already received a course of CBT for ED, it is recommended that the Stanford model be offered. This recommendation is somewhat tempered for patients with BN, as there are fewer research studies with this population. If an individual has a complex/co-morbid ED of any diagnosis, has not been helped by a course of EBT, demonstrates TIBs, or reports a high degree of emotional dysregulation, a program where their ED will be treated and conceptualized within the MED-DBT model is tentatively recommended. More research is needed on this model as there have been no RCTs in this area to date. Finally, if the patient has AN-R and has not been helped by other, more well-studied approaches, RO-DBT should be considered. It is important to note that since this model does not focus on eating and weight gain, this treatment, if attempted even experimentally, should be offered in the context of medical management. With any of these recommendations, the clinician is advised to adhere to a scientist-practitioner approach: Begin with what is known empirically to be effective, offer it to patients, evaluate progress, make changes in the context of consultation from other professionals, and present the outcomes. In doing so, the field continues to move forward and improved treatments options become available to adults with EDs.

ORCID

Fragiskos Gonidakis http://orcid.org/0000-0001-8212-280X
Emilio J. Compte http://orcid.org/0000-0002-6803-5950

References

Arnow, B., Kenardy, J., & Agras, W. S. (1992). Binge eating among the obese: A descriptive study. *Journal of Behavioral Medicine, 15*, 155–170. doi:10.1007/BF00848323

Bankoff, S. M., Karpel, M. G., Forbes, H. E., & Pantalone, D. W. (2012). A systematic review of dialectical behavior therapy for the treatment of eating disorders. *Eating Disorders: The Journal of Treatment and Preventions, 20*, 196–215. doi:10.1080/10640266.2012.668478

Ben-Porath, D., Wisniewski, L., & Warren, M. (2009). Outcomes of a DBT day treatment program for eating disorders: Clinical and statistical significance. *Journal of Contemporary Psychotherapy, 40*, 115–123. doi:10.1007/s10879-009-9125-5

Ben-Porath, D. D., Federici, A., Wisniewski, L., & Warren, M. (2014). Dialectical behavior therapy: Does it bring about improvements in affect regulation in individuals with eating disorders? *Contemp Psychotherapy, 44*, 245–251. doi:10.1007/s10879-014-9271-2

Brown, T. A., Cusack, A., Anderson, L., Reilly, E. E., Berner, L. A., Wierenga, C. E., … Kaye, W. H. (2019a). Early versus later improvements in dialectical behavior therapy skills use and treatment outcome in eating disorders. *Cognitive Therapy and Research, 43*(4), 759–768. doi:10.1007/s10608-019-10006-1

Brown, T. A., Cusack, A., Anderson, L. K., Trim, J., Nakamura, T., Trunko, M. E., & Kaye, W. H. (2018). Efficacy of a partial hospital programme for adults with eating disorders. *European Eating Disorders Review, 26*(3), 241–252. doi:10.1002/erv.v26.3

Brown, T. A., Cusack, A., Berner, L. A., Anderson, L. K., Nakamura, T., Gomez, L., ... Kaye, W. H. (2019b). Emotion regulation difficulties during and after partial hospitalization treatment across eating disorders. *Behavior Therapy.* doi:10.1016/j.beth.2019.07.002

Carter, J. C., Kenny, T. E., Singleton, C., & Van Wijk, M., & Heath, O. (2019). Dialectical behaviour therapy self-help for binge-eating disorder: A randomized controlled study. *International Journal of Eating Disorders,* eat.23208. doi:10.1002/eat.23208

Chen, E. Y., Cacioppo, J., Fettich, K., Gallop, R., McCloskey, M. S., Olino, T., & Zeffiro, T. A. (2017). An adaptive randomized trial of dialectical behavior therapy and cognitive behavior therapy for binge-eating. *Psychological Medicine, 47*(4), 703–717. doi:10.1017/S0033291716002543

Chen, E. Y., Matthews, L., Allen, C., Kuo, J. R., & Linehan, M. M. (2008). Dialectical behavior therapy for clients with binge-eating disorder or bulimia nervosa and borderline personality disorder. *International Journal of Eating Disorders, 41*(6), 505–512. doi:10.1002/eat.v41:6

Chen, E. Y., Segal, K., Weissman, J., Zeffiro, T. A., Gallop, R., Linehan, M. M., ... Lynch, T. R. (2015). Adapting dialectical behavior therapy for outpatient adult anorexia nervosa—A pilot study. *International Journal of Eating Disorders, 48*(1), 123–132. doi:10.1002/eat.v48.1

Courbasson, C., Nishikawa, Y., & Dixon, L. (2012). Outcome of dialectical behaviour therapy for concurrent eating and substance use disorders. *Clinical Psychology & Psychotherapy, 19* (5), 434–449. doi:10.1002/cpp.748

Erb, S., Farmer, A., & Mehlenbeck, R. (2013). A condensed dialectical behavior therapy skills group for binge eating disorder: Overcoming winter challenges. *Journal of Cognitive Psychotherapy, 27*(4), 338–358. doi:10.1891/0889-8391.27.4.338

Fairburn, C. G. (2008). *Cognitive behavior therapy and eating disorders.* New York, NY: *Guilford Press.*

Federici, A., & Wisniewski, L. (2013). An intensive DBT program for patients with multi-diagnostic eating disorder presentations: A case series analysis. *International Journal of Eating Disorders, 46,* 322–331. doi:10.1002/eat.v46.4

Federici, A., Wisniewski, L., & Ben-Porath, D. D. (2012). Description of an intensive dialectical behavior therapy program for multidiagnostic clients with eating disorders. *Journal of Counseling & Development, 90*(3), 330–338. doi:10.1002/j.1556-6676.2012.00041.x

Geller, J., Cockell, S. J., Hewitt, P. L., Goldner, E. M., & Flett, G. L. (2000). Inhibited expression of negative emotions and interpersonal orientation in anorexia nervosa. *International Journal of Eating Disorders, 28,* 8–19. doi:10.1002/(ISSN)1098-108X

Harrison, A., O'Brien, N., Lopez, C., & Treasure, J. (2010). Sensitivity to reward and punishment in eating disorders. *Psychiatry Research, 177,* 1–11. doi:10.1016/j.psychres.2009.06.010

Harrison, A., Sullivan, S., Tchanturia, K., & Treasure, J. (2010). Emotional functioning in eating disorders: Attentional bias, emotion recognition and emotion regulation. *Psychol Medicine, 40*(11), 1887–1897. doi:10.1017/S0033291710000036

Haye, P. P. J., Bacaltchuk, J., & Stefano, S. (2009). Psychological treatments for bulimia nervosa and binging. *Cochrane Database of Systematic Reviews (Online), 4,* CD000562.

Heatherton, T. F., & Baumeister, R. F. (1991). Binge eating as escape from self-awareness. *Psychological Bulletin, 110*(1), 86–108. doi:10.1037/0033-2909.110.1.86

Hempel, R. J., Vanderbleek, E., & Lynch, T. R. (2018). Radically Open DBT: Targeting emotional loneliness in anorexia nervosa. *Eating Disorders: the Journal of Treatment and Prevention, 26*(1), 92–104. doi:10.1080/10640266.2018.1418268

Johnson, C., Tobin, D. L., & Dennis, A. (1990). Differences in treatment outcome between borderline and nonborderline bulimics at one-year follow-up. *International Journal of Eating Disorders, 9*(6), 617–627. doi:10.1002/(ISSN)1098-108X

Klein, A. S., Skinner, J. B., & Hawley, K. M. (2012). Adapted group-based dialectical behaviour therapy for binge eating in a practicing clinic: Clinical outcomes and attrition. *European Eating Disorders Review, 20*(3), 148–153. doi:10.1002/erv.2165

Kröger, C., Schweiger, U., Sipos, V., Kliem, S., Arnold, R., Schunert, T., & Reinecker, H. (2010). Dialectical behaviour therapy and an added cognitive behavioural treatment module for eating disorders in women with borderline personality disorder and anorexia nervosa or bulimia nervosa who failed to respond to previous treatments. An open trial with a 15-month follow-up. *Journal of Behavior Therapy and Experimental Psychiatry, 41* (4), 381–388. doi:10.1016/j.jbtep.2010.04.001

Lenz, A. S., Taylor, R., Fleming, M., & Serman, N. (2014). Effectiveness of dialectical behavior therapy for treating eating disorders. *Journal of Counseling & Development, 92*, 26–35. doi:10.1002/j.1556-6676.2014.00127.x

Linardon, J., Fairburn, C. G., Fitzsimmons-Craft, E. E., Wilfley, D. E., & Brennan, L. (2017). The empirical status of the third-wave behaviour therapies for the treatment of eating disorders: A systematic review. *Clinical Psychology Review, 58*, 125–140. doi:10.1016/j.cpr.2017.10.005

Linehan, M. M., Armstrong, H. E., Suarez, A., Allmon, D., & Heard, H. L. (1991). Cognitive-behavioral treatment of chronically parasuicidal borderline patients. *Archives of General Psychiatry, 48*(12), 1060–1064. doi:10.1001/archpsyc.1991.01810360024003

Linehan, M. M., & Chen, E. Y. (2005). Dialectical behavior therapy for eating disorders. In A. Freeman, S.H. Felgoise, C.M. Nezu, A.M. Nezu & M.A. Reinecke (Eds.), *Encyclopedia of cognitive behavior therapy* (pp. 168–171). New York, NY: Springer-Verlag.

Lynch, T. R., Gray, K. L. H., Hempel, R. J., Titley, M., Chen, E. Y., & O'Mahen, H. A. (2013). Radically open-dialectical behavior therapy for adult anorexia nervosa: Feasibility and outcomes from an inpatient program. *BMC Psychiatry, 13*. doi:10.1186/1471-244X-13-293

Masson, P. C., von Ranson, K. M., Wallace, L. M., & Safer, D. L. (2013). A randomized wait-list controlled pilot study of dialectical behaviour therapy guided self-help for binge eating disorder. *Behaviour Research and Therapy, 51*(11), 723–728. doi:10.1016/j.brat.2013.08.001

McKay, M., & Fanning, P. (2016). *Self-esteem: A proven program of cognitive techniques for assessing, improving, and maintain your self-esteem* (3rd ed.). Oakland, CA: New Harbinger Publications.

Mushquash, A. R., & McMahan, M. (2015). Dialectical behavior therapy skills training reduces binge eating among patients seeking weight-management services: Preliminary evidence. *Eating and Weight Disorders - Studies on Anorexia, Bulimia and Obesity, 20*(3), 415–418. doi:10.1007/s40519-015-0177-0

Navarro-Haro, M. V., Botella, M. V., Guillen, C., Moliner, V., Marco, R., Jorquera, H., … Garcia-Palacios, A. (2018). Dialectical behavior therapy in the treatment of borderline personality disorder and eating disorders comorbidity: A pilot study in a naturalistic setting. *Cognitive Therapy & Research, 182*, 135–140.

Palmer, R. L., Birchall, H., Damani, S., Gatward, N., McGrain, L., & Parker, L. (2003). A dialectical behavior therapy program for people with an eating disorder and borderline personality disorder: Description and outcome. *International Journal of Eating Disorders, 33*(3), 281–286. doi:10.1002/eat.10141

Polivy, J., & Herman, C. P. (1993). Etiology of binge eating: Psychological mechanisms. In C. G. Fairburn & G. T. Wilson (Eds.), *Binge eating: Nature, assessment, and treatment* (pp. 173–205). New York, NY: Guilford Press.

Rahmani, M., Omidi, A., Asemi, Z., & Akbari, H. (2018). The effect of dialectical behaviour therapy on binge eating, difficulties in emotion regulation and BMI in overweight patients with binge-eating disorder: A randomized controlled trial. *Mental Health & Prevention, 9*, 13–18. doi:10.1016/j.mhp.2017.11.002

Robinson, A. H., & Safer, D. L. (2012). Moderators of dialectical behavior therapy for binge eating disorder: Results from a randomized controlled trial. *International Journal of Eating Disorders, 45*(4), 597–602. doi:10.1002/eat.20932

Rossier, V., Bolognini, M., Plancherel, B., & Halfon, O. (2000). Sensation seeking: A personality trait characteristic of adolescent girls and young women with eating disorders? *European Eating Disorders Review, 8*, 245–252. doi:10.1002/(ISSN)1099-0968

Safer, D. L., Adler, S., & Masson, P. C. (2018). *The DBT solution for emotional eating: The DBT solution for emotional eating: A proven program to break the cycle of bingeing and out-of control eating*. New York, NY: Guilford Press.

Safer, D. L., Lively, T. J., Telch, C. F., & Agras, W. S. (2002). Predictors of relapse following successful dialectical behavior therapy for binge eating disorder. *International Journal of Eating Disorders, 32*(2), 155–163. doi:10.1002/(ISSN)1098-108X

Safer, D. L., Robinson, A. H., & Jo, B. (2010). Outcome from a randomized controlled trial of group therapy for binge eating disorder: Comparing dialectical behavior therapy adapted for binge eating to an active comparison group therapy. *Behavior Therapy, 41*(1), 106–120. doi:10.1016/j.beth.2009.01.006

Safer, D. L., Telch, C. F., & Agras, W. S. (2001). Dialectical behavior therapy for bulimia nervosa. *American Journal of Psychiatry, 158*(4), 632–634. doi:10.1176/appi.ajp.158.4.632

Safer, D. L., Telch, C. F., & Chen, E. Y. (2009). *Dialectical behavior therapy for binge eating and bulimia*. New York, NY: The Guilford Press.

Tchanturia, K., Harrison, A., Nakazato, M., Schmidt, U., … Morris, R. (2012). Poor cognitive flexibility in eating disorders: Examining the evidence using the wisconsin card sorting task. *PLoS ONE, 7*(1), e28331. doi:10.1371/journal.pone.0028331

Telch, C. F., Agras, W. S., & Linehan, M. M. (2000). Group dialectical behavior therapy for binge-eating disorder: A preliminary, uncontrolled trial. *Behavior Therapy, 31*(3), 569–582. doi:10.1016/S0005-7894(00)80031-3

Telch, C. F., Agras, W. S., & Linehan, M. M. (2001). Dialectical behavior therapy for binge eating disorder. *Journal of Consulting and Clinical Psychology, 69*(6), 1061–1065. doi:10.1037/0022-006X.69.6.1061

Waller, G. (2003). The psychology of binge eating. In C. G. Fairburn & K. D. Brownell (Eds.), *Eating disorders and obesity: A comprehensive handbook* (pp. 98–102). New York, NY: Guilford Press.

Wiser, S., & Telch, C. F. (1999). Dialectical behavior therapy for binge-eating disorder. *Journal of Clinical Psychology, 55*(6), 755–768. doi:10.1002/(ISSN)1097-4679

Wisniewski, L., & Ben-Porath, D. D. (2015). Dialectical behavior therapy and eating disorders: The use of contingency management procedures to manage dialectical dilemmas. *American Journal of Psychotherapy, 69*, 129–140. doi:10.1176/appi.psychotherapy.2015.69.2.129

Wisniewski, L., & Kelly, E. (2003). The application of dialectical behavior therapy to the treatment of eating disorders. *Cognitive and Behavioral Practice, 10*(2), 131–138. doi:10.1016/S1077-7229(03)80021-4

Zucker, N. L., Losh, N., Bulik, C. M., LaBar, K. S., Piven, J., & Pelphery, K. A. (2007). Anorexia nervosa and autism spectrum disorders: Guided investigation of social cognitive endophenotypes. *Psychological Bulletin, 133*, 99–1006. doi:10.1037/0033-2909.133.6.976

Dialectical behavioral therapy for the treatment of adolescent eating disorders: a review of existing work and proposed future directions

Erin E. Reilly, Natalia C. Orloff, Tana Luo, Laura A. Berner, Tiffany A. Brown, Kimberly Claudat, Walter H. Kaye, and Leslie K. Anderson

ABSTRACT

Over the past several decades, Dialectical Behavior Therapy (DBT) has been adapted for a range of presenting problems related to emotion dysregulation. Considerable enthusiasm exists regarding the use of DBT for treating eating disorders; however, to date, there have been no reviews summarizing empirical efforts to adapt DBT for eating disorders in youth. Accordingly, in the present narrative review, we provide a comprehensive summary of existing work testing DBT for adolescent eating disorders. First, we briefly review existing work applying DBT to eating disorders in adults and general adolescent samples. We then review research focused specifically on the use of DBT for adolescent eating disorders, including both those studies applying DBT as the primary treatment and investigations of DBT as an adjunctive treatment. Overall, initial results for DBT-based approaches are promising. However, rigorous empirical work testing DBT for treating adolescent eating disorders remains limited; the majority of existing research is comprised of case series and small-scale studies. Therefore, we close with specific recommendations for future research testing this approach.

Introduction

Eating disorders, including anorexia nervosa (AN) and bulimia nervosa (BN), commonly begin in adolescence and are associated with marked functional impairment, serious medical consequences, and increased risk of death (Arcelus et al., 2011; Mitchell & Crow, 2006). For adolescent AN, Family-Based Treatment (FBT; Lock, Le Grange, Agras & Dare, 2001) has demonstrated efficacy in randomized controlled trials (RCTs) and effectiveness in naturalistic research designs (Couturier et al., 2013). However, up to 50% of adolescents with AN who receive FBT do not experience full remission of symptoms (J. Lock et al., 2010). Further, outcome data on FBT for the treatment of BN are somewhat mixed (Le Grange et al., 2007, 2015). Therefore, in light of the well-documented burden associated with eating disorders and their consequences in children, adolescents, and their families (e.g., Zabala et al., 2009), there remains a pressing need to identify adjunctive or alternative treatments.

Dialectical Behavior Therapy (DBT) has received attention in the literature as one promising alternative treatment option for adolescent eating disorders. Originally developed for use in chronically suicidal individuals with Borderline Personality Disorder (BPD), DBT outlines a clear framework for treating emotional and behavioral dysregulation common in multi-problem, complex patients, using a combination of individual therapy, skills groups, phone coaching, and therapist consultation (Linehan, 1991). Skills conferred in therapy are grouped into four modules, including distress tolerance, emotion regulation, mindfulness, and interpersonal effectiveness (Linehan, 1991). Several RCTs have documented the efficacy of DBT for treating individuals with chronic suicidal behaviors and BPD (e.g., M. M. Linehan et al., 2006, 2015). Over the past 30 years, DBT has been adapted for a number of populations, including adolescents with emotion dysregulation and their families (Miller et al., 2009) and adults with eating disorders (e.g., Telch et al., 2001). Those who support the application of DBT to eating disorders highlight data suggesting that eating disorders are associated with high levels of emotion dysregulation (Haynos & Fruzzetti, 2011; Lavender et al., 2015) and often present in conjunction with other impulsive, dysregulated behaviors, such as substance use and non-suicidal self-injury (NSSI; Fischer & Grange, 2007; Peebles et al., 2011).

Moreover, in theory, DBT may be well suited to target several adolescent populations who have a poor response to FBT. For instance, higher levels of parental expressed emotion and criticism are associated with worse FBT outcome (e.g., Rienecke et al., 2016, 2017). Elevated familial expressed emotion and invalidation have also been implicated in adolescent suicidal behaviors and emotion dysregulation (Sim et al., 2009); accordingly, DBT for adolescents includes a focus on increasing validation and effective family communication (Miller et al., 2009), which may also be helpful for patients with eating disorders. While there has been increasing interest in adapting DBT for eating disorders, to our knowledge, there are no existing empirical reviews of DBT for eating disorders in youth.

Thus, we aim to (a) summarize existing work exploring the usefulness of DBT for the treatment of adolescent eating disorders, both as a stand-alone and an adjunctive treatment, and (b) delineate a roadmap for future research in this domain. To achieve these goals, we place existing work in context by briefly outlining research on DBT for adult eating disorders and adolescents with emotion regulation difficulties and suicidality. Next, we provide a comprehensive narrative review of work testing the effectiveness of DBT, alone and in conjunction with FBT, for adolescent eating disorders. Finally, we highlight the limitations of existing knowledge and propose next steps for this area of research. Of note, throughout the current paper, we will use the term "adapted" when significant changes were made to the treatment delivery or content and the term "modified" when minor changes were made to the treatment.

DBT for eating disorders: findings from adult samples

Efforts to implement DBT with adolescents with eating disorders have drawn significantly upon initial attempts to apply this treatment with adult eating disorder patients. Given the initial development of DBT for adults with BPD, several studies have evaluated full-package DBT for eating disorders comorbid with BPD (Palmer et al., 2003; Navarro-Haro et al., 2018). Most of the research on DBT for adult eating disorders without BPD has focused on bulimia and binge eating disorder (Rahmani, Omidi, Asemi, & Akbari, 2018; Safer & Jo, 2010; Telch et al., 2000). However, recent research has also evaluated DBT as a treatment approach for eating disorders characterized by emotional and behavioral overcontrol, such as the restricting subtype of AN (AN-R) using Radically Open-DBT (RO-DBT) (Lynch, Gray, Hempel, Titley, Chen, & O'Mahen, 2013). Various adaptations and modifications of DBT have also been evaluated in adult samples, including DBT integrated with appetite awareness training (Hill et al., 2011), DBT for obese emotional eaters (Roosen, Safer, Cebolla, & van Strien, 2012), and modified DBT for women with full or sub-threshold Binge Eating Disorder (BED) or BN (Klein et al., 2013). To help increase the accessibility of DBT, research has begun to examine guided self-help DBT for adult BED (Masson et al., 2013).

Overall, eight studies have tested DBT for adult eating disorders using randomized designs (Ben-Porath et al., this issue), most often using wait-list control groups and focusing on bulimic spectrum eating disorders. To date, two meta-analyses have examined DBT for adults with eating disorders. Linardon et al. (2017) conducted a meta-analysis on RCTs of third-wave behavioral therapies, including DBT, and concluded that DBT was "possibly efficacious" for the treatment of BN and BED. With slightly more broad inclusion criteria, Lenz et al. (2014) evaluated nine studies utilizing between- and within-subjects designs, and results indicated a large effect size for DBT. These preliminary findings in support of DBT for adults with eating disorders provide compelling rationale for evaluating the applicability of DBT to adolescent eating disorders.

General adaptation of DBT for adolescents

The first adaptation of DBT for adolescents (Miller et al., 1997) included family members and teens, changed the length of treatment to 12 weeks, used simplified, teen-appropriate language to describe skills, and reduced the total number of skills taught compared to adult DBT. Following an initial promising quasi-experimental test of this modified program in suicidal adolescents with features of BPD (Rathus & Miller, 2002), Miller and colleagues published the first manual describing DBT for suicidal adolescents (Miller et al., 2009), which has subsequently been updated (Rather & Miller, 2015). This manual includes 24 weeks of treatment, individual therapy, multi-family skills groups, phone coaching for both adolescent patients and their family members, family sessions as needed, an as-needed graduate group with other treatment modes, and one additional skills training module called "walking the middle path" that focuses on validation, behavioral principles, and adolescent-family dialectical dilemmas. Currently, two RCTs have tested full-package DBT for adolescents with NSSI and features of BPD (McCauley et al., 2018; Mehlum et al., 2014). Results indicate that DBT is associated with significant reductions in NSSI, suicide attempts, suicidal ideation, and depression scores. Follow-up data suggest that DBT remained superior to enhanced usual care in reducing NSSI at one-year post-treatment (Mehlum et al., 2016).

Most studies on adolescent DBT have focused on BPD features and NSSI. As a result, the first, and currently only, meta-analysis of DBT for adolescents focuses on depressive symptoms and NSSI (Cook & Gorraiz, 2016). Twelve studies were included in the final analysis, and results indicate that DBT has a large effect on NSSI and a small effect on depression. Of note, these studies differed in terms of elements of DBT used (e.g., skills group only, individual therapy and skills group, alternating sessions of family skills training and individual therapy, use of phone coaching and diary cards). Additionally, none of the studies included in this meta-analysis were RCTs, only five included control groups, and few reported on therapist adherence.

Although the only existing meta-analysis of adolescent DBT focuses on depressive symptoms and NSSI, two comprehensive narrative reviews have included adolescent-focused adaptations of DBT that have targeted a wide range of symptom presentations. Groves et al. (2012) reviewed findings from 12 studies, and MacPherson et al. (2013) reviewed the results of 18 studies across differing presenting problems. Overall, these reviews suggest DBT for adolescents is acceptable and associated with relatively high rates of retention. Moreover, the authors conclude that the reviewed studies provide some empirical support for DBT in reducing hospitalizations, suicidality, and NSSI behavior in adolescents, as well as reducing symptoms of depression, bipolar disorder, eating disorders, and other impulsive behaviors. Given that studies through 2013 included a broad range of milieus, patient populations, and modalities, but no RCTs, Groves et al. (2012) and MacPherson et al. (2013) all conclude that there is evidence for the practical effectiveness of DBT for adolescents, particularly those that struggle with emotion dysregulation and impulsivity. These authors also underscore the utility of DBT-based approaches in community outpatient, school, or residential settings that treat youth with multiple problems. These assertions have since been further supported by effectiveness studies of DBT for high-risk adolescents in community clinic settings (e.g., Berk et al., 2019).

Taken together, the majority of existing work examining DBT for adolescents has focused on youth with features of BPD, including NSSI and suicide attempts, and suggests that DBT effectively targets these symptoms. However, reviews also indicate that DBT approaches adapted and modified for other adolescent populations characterized by emotion dysregulation (e.g., incarcerated populations, community mental health patients) show considerable, albeit tentative, promise and warrant further investigation.

DBT for adolescent eating disorders

The success of DBT for adolescents and initial evidence documenting efficacy in adult populations with eating disorders (e.g., Bankoff et al., 2012; MacPherson et al., 2013) has laid the groundwork for incorporating this intervention into adolescent eating disorder treatments. However, the manner in which DBT has been included in these treatments varies considerably. In the current review, we chose to include all studies that have tested DBT as either the primary or an adjunctive intervention and included adolescents (<18 years old) who presented with eating disorders as a primary treatment target. Given that this area of research remains limited, we were broad in our inclusion of study designs (e.g., open trials; case studies). We separate our review of existing literature into two sections (see Table 1): studies using DBT as the main treatment approach for adolescent eating disorders and studies exploring the use of DBT as an adjunctive treatment.

DBT for adolescents as the primary protocol

To date, four studies have tested DBT as the main protocol for adolescent eating disorders. These studies are heterogeneous in their design (e.g., pilot studies, case reports), level of care (e.g., outpatient, inpatient), and sample characteristics (e.g., AN, BN, BED), and are detailed below.

Salbach-Andrae et al. (2007, 2008) published a pilot study and case series examining the effectiveness of DBT for adolescent eating disorders. The authors' (2007) pilot included 31 adolescent girls diagnosed with AN (n = 23) or BN (n = 8) who were enrolled in an inpatient program. Participants received DBT treatment based on the existing adolescent DBT manual (Miller et al., 2009, 1997), with several adaptations. Specifically, the treatment was shorter in duration, but included more frequent sessions, was delivered by both therapists and nurses, and included eating disorder-specific content (e.g., weight- and eating-focused groups). Results indicated that, from pre- to post-treatment, the full sample evidenced significant decreases in eating disorder behaviors and

Table 1. Existing studies: DBT for adolescent eating disorders.

Study	Sample	Follow-Up?	Setting	Treatment Approach	Adaptations	Findings
DBT as Primary Treatment						
Salbach-Andrae et al. (2008)	N = 31; Adolescents with AN, BN	No	Inpatient	DBT program including individual and group-based sessions	Modifications to Miller's treatment model; shortened duration of treatment, increased frequency of sessions; utilized therapists and nurse staff to deliver treatment; addition of weekly groups focused on eating and weight	97.4% retention; increase in BMI in AN patients; decrease in depression symptoms, eating disorder behavior, and use of weight-loss substances
Salbach-Andrae et al. (2008)	N = 12 Adolescents with AN, BN	No	Outpatient	25-week program: individual sessions; phone coaching, weekly skills group; family members attend 8 skills groups; therapist consultation	Shortened Miller's protocol; addition of eating disorder-specific module and adolescent general DBT module (Walking the Middle Path); family component for skills group	92% retention; decreases in eating disorder symptoms, associated symptoms (EDI-II subscales), and improvements in functional impairment
Safer et al., 2007	N = 1; Adolescent with BED	Yes	Outpatient	21-week program including individual sessions focusing on DBT skills, diary card review, and behavioral chains of binge eating behaviors; 4 family sessions; phone coaching	No group component; increased emphasis on homework in sessions; scheduling calls if patient reticent to use phone coaching; family component for sessions if indicated by chains	Reduction from 22 OBEs in month before treatment to 4 OBEs in final month of treatment; reductions in EDE scores; at 3-month follow-up, 1 OBE reported in last 3 months
Fischer & Peterson (2015)	10 adolescents with BN or EDNOS & suicidal behaviors	Yes	Outpatient	6-month treatment program; weekly skills training, individual session, weekly therapist consultation telephone coaching between sessions; parents attended 1 session every month; parent-specific skills groups made available	Included psychoeducation on eating disorders; family component in the form of attending individual sessions and option for family skills sessions (only 3/7 attended)	70% retention; significant reductions in eating disorder behaviors and cognitive symptoms (as measured by EDE); significant decreases in self-injury; these effects maintained at 6-month follow-up

(Continued)

Table 1. (Continued).

Study	Sample	Follow-Up?	Setting	Treatment Approach	Adaptations	Findings
DBT as Adjunctive Treatment						
Johnston et al. (2015)	51 adolescents with AN, BN, EDNOS	Yes	Intensive Outpatient	7-8-week program, comprised of 3 hours a day, 3 days/week; DBT skills groups; parents skill group (1x/week); group/family meals; other adjunctive groups; family sessions focused on FBT interventions	Skills groups organized in 8-week curriculum; separated into "DBT Skills Integration," "Multi-Family Group for Walking the Middle Path," "Emotion Regulation/Mindfulness," "Distress Tolerance/Interpersonal Effectiveness," "DBT Problem Solving," and "Parent DBT"	71% treatment retention; significant increases in IBW during treatment, continued to increase at 3-, 6- and 12-month follow-up; significant decreases in EDE-Q scores, continued to improve at 6- and 12-month follow-up; no significant changes in binge/purge symptoms in treatment or at follow-up.
Murray et al. (2015)	35 adolescents with BN	No	Partial Hospital/ Intensive Outpatient	Interventions delivered up to 6 days a week between 3–10 hours daily; individual sessions followed DBT protocol; family sessions followed FBT protocol; parent-only group focused on behavioral management; multi-family DBT component	DBT groups adapted to include all family members and extended into multi-family meals.	Only evaluated completers; decreases in EDE-Q scores for 1) shape concerns, 2) weight concerns, and 3) global scores; significant reductions in frequency of 1) secretive eating, 2) objective binges, 3) self-induced vomiting; significant improvement in emotion regulation strategies and parents' report of self-efficacy in treating the eating disorder
Pennell et al. (2019)	24 adolescents with AN-R, AN-BP, BN, OSFED, ARFID	Yes	Partial Hospital Program	Contracted 6 weeks minimum; 5 day/week program, with attendance being 10 hours 4x/week and 7 hours 1x/week; patient skills groups 2-3x/day focused on DBT modules; completion of diary cards, chain analyses, skills homework; other adjunctive groups; daily family meals; weekend planning family group; family session focused on FBT interventions	DBT modules split into 1) Distress Tolerance Skills, 2) Emotion Regulation and Interpersonal Skills, 3) Mindfulness, 4) Distress Tolerance/Weekend Family Planning; Patients in separate "skills practice" and "coping skills" groups daily	79.2% retention; significant increases in weight at discharge; Reports of reduction or abstinence of B/P behaviors at discharge; 79.2% remained out of the hospital at 2-year follow up

(Continued)

Table 1. (Continued).

Study	Sample	Follow-Up?	Setting	Treatment Approach	Adaptations	Findings
Peterson et al. (2019)	18 adolescents with AN-R, AN-BP, OSFED	No	Outpatient	6-month program; DBT skills groups for adolescents followed 24-week Standard Adult DBT Skills Training Schedule (2 weeks mindfulness, 6 weeks distress tolerance, 2 weeks mindfulness, 7 week emotion regulation, 2 weeks mindfulness, 5 weeks interpersonal effectiveness); additional elements of traditional DBT: mindfulness activity, diary card, homework review, etc.	No adaptation to traditional DBT skills group	66.6% retention; large effect size for increase in adaptive skills, decrease in dysfunctional coping strategies, small to medium effect sizes for decrease in objective binge episodes and in percentage of expected body weight; small effect sizes in decreases in global and restraint scores on the EDE-Q; diary cards indicated a decreasing trend in target behaviors at week 9 and increase at week 17 and an overall increase in skill usage

cognitive symptoms, and individuals with AN demonstrated significant increases in body mass index (BMI).

The second study by Salbach-Andrae et al. (2008) evaluated DBT for adolescent eating disorders (AN-R; AN-BP; BN) in an outpatient setting (N = 12). Adaptations to Miller, Rathus and Linehan's (2009) protocol for DBT with adolescents included the addition of a module focused specifically on eating, weight, and body image, entitled "Dealing with Food and Body Image." Treatment goals were established following the traditional DBT hierarchy. Results supported reductions in eating disorder symptoms including binge eating, vomiting, other compensatory behaviors, and restriction, as well as general psychopathology, pre- to post-treatment. Of the 11 adolescents who completed treatment, five (four AN-R and one AN-BP) did not meet criteria for an eating disorder at the end of 25-week treatment, two BN patients had diagnostic crossover and met criteria for Eating Disorder Not Otherwise Specified (EDNOS), and the remaining four retained their initial diagnosis, one with AN-BP and three with BN.

One case study explored the use of DBT for the treatment of a 16-year-old adolescent with BED (Safer et al., 2007). Safer and colleagues presented a 21-week individual treatment protocol that closely mirrored the existing DBT protocol for adult BED. Sessions using this model included a review of diary cards, behavioral chains, between-session phone coaching, and acquisition and practice of skills covering the four modules. Parental involvement was based on feedback from patient diary cards and behavioral chains. Case study results suggested a decrease in binge eating episodes from pre-treatment to follow-up, with 28 episodes at pre-treatment, 4 at post-treatment, and 1 at follow-up.

Fischer and Peterson (2015) published the most recent 6-month pilot study of DBT in an outpatient setting for adolescents with BN and also engaged in NSSI. Notably, this duration of treatment aligns with that of Salbach's outpatient case series, which was 25 weeks. Patients received psychoeducation on eating disorders, as an adjunct to the traditional psychoeducation on the biosocial model of emotion dysregulation employed during traditional DBT (Linehan, 1991). Elements of traditional Cognitive-Behavioral Therapy (CBT) were also included in the first two psychoeducation sessions. In addition, adolescents enrolled in the study attended weekly individual sessions, participated in weekly skills training groups, received phone coaching, and identified treatment goals based on the DBT hierarchy. However, unlike Miller's model and Salbach's (2007) DBT adaptation, families in this pilot were involved in a systematic fashion, such that parents and/or legal guardians attended the initial assessment, one monthly joint family session, and were able to attend a parent skills group. The sample studied were adolescent females (n = 10) with a diagnosis of BN or EDNOS and suicidal behavior. Unlike the samples studied by Salbach-Andrae et al. (2008, 2008), the majority of participants were overweight or obese at intake. Seven of the ten participants completed treatment; results suggested a decrease in cognitive eating disorder symptoms, binge eating, purging, and NSSI at post-treatment and at 6-month follow-up. Three individuals reported complete absence of binge eating behaviors at 6-month follow-up.

The limited data on DBT as the primary intervention for eating disorders in an adolescent population tentatively supports potential benefits. However, given the large variability in the sample characteristics, treatment settings, manner in which DBT was implemented, and lack of generalizable treatment designs (i.e., primarily use of case series), the definitive conclusions that can be drawn from the existing work are limited.

DBT as an adjunct to FBT

Given the status of FBT as the first-line treatment for adolescent eating disorders, it is not surprising that interest in DBT as an adjunctive treatment for adolescents has focused primarily on pairing DBT with FBT. Although evidence suggests that emotion dysregulation and impulsive behaviors are common in adolescent eating disorders (Fischer & Peterson, 2015), the standard FBT protocol does not provide any guidance regarding targeting these behaviors in family sessions. Accordingly, researchers have proposed that an integration of FBT and DBT may provide a framework for targeting eating disorder behaviors and associated emotional features (Anderson et al., 2015; Federici & Wisniewski, 2012). Exploration of theoretically merging these two treatment approaches has highlighted the overlap in key aspects of treatment, such as a non-judgmental stance, encouraging separation between the patient and the illness, a focus on decreasing maladaptive behaviors, and facilitating an environment of validation and acceptance during the refeeding process (Anderson et al., 2015; Federici & Wisniewski, 2012). On the other hand, there are several notable philosophical differences between the treatments, including the conceptualization of eating pathology from an agnostic versus biosocial perspective, the role of the therapist in session, level of family involvement, and overall theorized mechanisms of change. Indeed, FBT posits eating disorder behaviors emerge from ambivalence and neurobiological vulnerabilities, while DBT maintains that behaviors are in response to a lack of skill in managing one's affective states (Anderson et al., 2015; Federici & Wisniewski, 2012). Nonetheless, these authors outline ways that these differences may be resolved and propose that the two approaches can be complementary in comprehensively targeting adolescent eating disorders.

Several research teams have presented preliminary data on the integration of FBT and DBT (Johnston et al., 2015; Murray et al., 2015; Pennell et al., 2019; Peterson et al., 2019). First, Murray and colleagues (2015) tested the short-term outcomes associated with a blended FBT and DBT approach in a sample of adolescents with BN (n = 35). Participants were enrolled in a combined partial hospital and intensive outpatient program and received weekly FBT alongside individual, family, multi-family, and parent-only DBT, as outlined by Anderson et al. (2015). The length of treatment varied across participants and was determined by illness severity and progress toward therapeutic targets. Results at post-treatment indicated a decrease in cognitive eating disorder symptoms, decreased shape and weight concerns, and overall improvement in emotion regulation strategies. Parents also reported an increase in efficacy in assisting their child with their eating disorder symptoms.

Johnston et al. (2015) explored the outcomes associated with a blended FBT-DBT approach administered in an intensive-outpatient setting but extended this work by evaluating outcomes of this program at one-year follow-up. Adolescents (n = 51) diagnosed with either AN, BN, or EDNOS received weekly FBT sessions and DBT groups in both separated adolescent/parent and multi-family formats. The DBT groups (both individual and multi-family format) utilized a combination of traditional DBT modules (M. M. Linehan, 1993; Miller et al., 2009) and DBT-based didactics adapted for eating disorders. Results from the open trial suggested significant improvement in BMI and cognitive symptoms, post-treatment. Follow-up data suggested that eating disorder symptoms continued to decrease through 6-month follow-up, and BMI continued to increase at 1-year follow-up. Of note, while it has been hypothesized that DBT skills would be effective in interrupting the pattern of dysregulation and maladaptive behaviors (Anderson et al., 2015) related to BN, results indicated no significant changes in binge eating and purging frequency throughout treatment or at 1-year follow-up.

Third, Peterson et al. (2019) conducted an open trial of manualized weekly FBT for AN with adjunctive weekly DBT skills training groups for a sample of 18 adolescents with AN-R over the course of 24 weeks. Results indicated that participants reported an increase in adaptive skills, decreases in cognitive eating disorder symptoms, decreases in levels of restraint, and decreases in depressive symptomatology. Data from weekly diary cards indicated a decrease in behavioral targets at week 9, but a rebound of behaviors at week 17. Despite this rebound, which is hypothesized to be due to the module being covered at that time (interpersonal effectiveness) not providing skills to directly target behaviors, there was an overall reduction in eating disorder behaviors at post-treatment (Peterson et al., 2019).

Finally, Pennell et al. (2019) outlined the outcomes of another FBT-DBT blended approach, implemented in a partial hospitalization sample (n = 24, 83% received FBT and DBT). The sample was comprised of adolescents diagnosed with AN-R, AN-BP, BN, Other Specified Eating Disorder, and Avoidant/Restrictive Food Intake Disorder (ARFID). In terms of the treatment approach, FBT was implemented as outlined by Lock and LeGrange (2013), with Phase I or Phase II treatment techniques used depending on the severity of illness (Lock & LeGrange, 2013). DBT interventions included daily skills groups, skills practice, diary card completion, and behavioral analysis. Results at discharge indicated significant increases in weight among low-weight eating disorders and significant decreases in binge eating and purging behaviors. The authors also noted that readmission rates during the study period were low.

Altogether, studies exploring the integration of DBT and FBT suggest that this adjunctive approach is both feasible and may provide benefit. However, these studies are few in number and have several major limitations, including lack of follow-up data, small sample sizes, and non-randomized designs.

Summary of existing work and future directions

Despite the fact that DBT or its components (e.g., skills groups) are commonly offered as part of treatment packages delivered in higher levels of care for eating disorders, our review of existing literature indicates that there remain few studies exploring the empirical basis of DBT for adolescent eating disorders. In the following sections, we offer recommendations for future research exploring the efficacy and effectiveness of this approach and attempting to characterize the individuals for whom and the contexts in which DBT provides maximal utility.

Recommendations for future research on DBT for adolescent eating disorders

First and foremost, given that existing studies of DBT for eating disorders have been conducted in small samples and have employed naturalistic designs, it is critical that researchers conduct RCTs of DBT for eating disorders in youth. Further, given the significant lack of consistency in the nuances of DBT applications in existing adolescent work, it is recommended that efforts to test DBT for adolescent eating disorders standardize treatment application and choice of outcome assessment whenever possible to facilitate comparisons across studies. Finally, in light of recent meta-scientific inquiry highlighting quality-related issues with many existing empirical reports for evidence-based treatments (e.g., Sakaluk et al., 2019), we recommend that future research make use of multi-site or multi-lab designs to increase statistical power and follow proposed open science guidelines to increase the evidentiary quality of treatment-related research (e.g., preregistering projects and analyses; increasing transparency in reporting; e.g., Tackett et al., 2017).

Moderators: for whom is DBT most effective?

Following the initial determination of efficacy and effectiveness of DBT for adolescent eating disorders, it will be important to determine for whom DBT may be best suited. We recommend that researchers and clinicians use existing moderator research in DBT for other presenting problems (e.g., Sahin et al., 2018) as a starting point for determining for whom DBT is most effective. We also recommend that researchers and clinicians consider a range of clinical characteristics—diagnostic, demographic, developmental, or psychological—that may indicate or contraindicate the use of DBT or influence outcome. When considering potential moderators of treatment, existing work in adolescents has explored the application of DBT across different eating disorder diagnoses (AN, BN, BED). Although there is a theoretical reason to believe that emotion dysregulation may be implicated across diagnostic presentations (e.g., Haynos & Fruzzetti, 2011; Lavender et al., 2015), future work should directly test whether DBT is best suited to target eating disorder presentations characterized by affective lability and negative urgency (Anestis et al., 2009; Waxman, 2009), as has been implicated in more general adaptations of DBT (Zapolski & Smith, 2017), or whether eating disorders characterized by over-controlled temperamental characteristics and restricting behaviors (i.e., AN-R) also derive benefit.

Relatedly, specific to adolescent and family-based implementations of DBT, future work should consider developmental or family-based factors that could influence the appropriateness or effects of DBT. For instance, given the emphasis on improving emotion-related communication and validation in adolescent adaptations of DBT (e.g., Miller et al., 2009), it may be that families with dysfunction in these domains (e.g., high levels of expressed emotion and criticism) would benefit most from DBT.

With regard to developmental characteristics, studies of DBT for adolescents with eating disorders have included patients as young as 12, but research suggests that earlier intervention is associated with improved outcome in eating disorders (e.g., Treasure & Russell, 2011). Preliminary data from an RCT for Disruptive Mood Dysregulation Disorder indicate that DBT adapted for preadolescent patients (DBT-C; Perepletchikova et al., 2011) is nearly twice as acceptable and efficacious as an active psychosocial and medication management control condition for children as young as 7 years old (Perepletchikova et al., 2017). Preadolescents with NSSI, suicidality, and severe emotional and behavioral dysregulation were included in the study. Given that these comorbidities can also characterize children with eating disorders, future work investigating DBT-C for pediatric AN, BN, ARFID, and BED is also needed.

Finally, almost all existing work on DBT has included predominantly white, female samples. It will be critical for future work to explore the usefulness of DBT for varying demographic groups and test any efforts to adapt the administration of DBT to include considerations specific to these adolescent groups and their families.

Cost-effectiveness analyses

Because DBT is a multi-faceted and comprehensive treatment approach that requires extensive therapist training, cost-effective analyses are also helpful to evaluate its effects relative to other treatments (Wilkinson, 2018). Economic analyses have been conducted for adult DBT (M. M. Linehan et al., 1999), but not for adolescent DBT. Particularly given the high cost of eating disorder treatment (Striegel-Moore et al., 2000) and the added cost for adolescent treatment if family members travel to participate in treatment, we suggest that future research explore questions related to cost-effectiveness of adolescent DBT for eating disorders.

Component analysis

Although adherent DBT takes a multi-pronged approach to treatment, including individual therapy sessions, group sessions, telephone coaching, and therapist consultation, it is common for adaptations of DBT to exclude one or more of these components for theoretical or logistical reasons. For this reason, it is critical that future research conduct component analyses of DBT that explore the utility of these different components across differing presenting problems. Recent component analyses of DBT for adult BPD suggest that a range of DBT formats are associated with overall benefit, but that skills groups may be particularly important for the outcome (M. M. Linehan et al., 2015). Of note, these questions may be particularly useful in extending past work for DBT in adult eating disorders and adolescents, as the majority of existing work in DBT for adult eating disorders has used group-only formats and adolescent DBT protocols often add additional elements related to family involvement (e.g., family sessions). We recommend that future research on DBT for adolescents explore the effectiveness of each component, as this will be useful in streamlining dissemination.

Mechanisms of change in DBT

A more general question of interest to both DBT for adolescent eating disorders and DBT more broadly concerns the mechanisms of treatment change. In particular, few existing studies have empirically tested mediators of treatment change in DBT, or mechanisms through which the treatment achieves its positive effects. Identifying mechanisms of change is an important priority for research on psychological treatments and can guide intervention delivery in a manner that maximizes efficacy (Kazdin, 2007). Lynch et al. (2006) proposed a number of potential mechanisms theoretically relevant to DBT, including exposure and response prevention, enhanced learning of new effective responses to emotionally salient cues, enhanced attentional control, memory, and stimulus discrimination. The authors highlight that the majority of proposed mechanisms can be summarized as relating to the promotion of new learning and shifting from ineffective to effective action tendencies in response to strong emotions (Lynch et al., 2006). To date, few studies have empirically tested these proposed mechanisms; one RCT of DBT for women with BPD suggested that increases in effective skills use was a mechanism of change for a range of outcomes (Neacsiu et al., 2010). Two recent studies in adult eating disorders supported a similar role of skills use in accounting for eating disorder-related treatment outcome (Brown et al., 2018) and changes in affect regulation over the course of group-based DBT for eating disorders (Ben-Porath et al., 2014), providing some initial support for the hypothesized mechanisms outlined by Lynch et al. (2006). Overall, the literature exploring proposed mechanisms of change in DBT is sparse; we recommend that efforts to provide empirical backing of DBT for adolescent eating disorders include assessments gauging proposed mechanisms of change, including both processes implicated in general delivery of DBT, as well as family-related processes that may be implicated in adolescent-specific adaptations of DBT.

Conclusions

In the 30 years since DBT was first outlined by Marsha Linehan (M. M. Linehan, 1987), there has been widespread interest in applying its theoretical model and intervention strategies to treat a wide range of presenting problems linked to emotion dysregulation (Dimeff, & Koerner, 2007), including eating disorders (e.g., Safer & Jo, 2010). Although initial RCTs in adults and pilot tests in adolescent samples support the promise of DBT for the treatment of eating disordered behaviors, ongoing research is necessary to provide rigorous evidence for the use of this approach and explore the populations and contexts for which it is best suited.

Acknowledgments

Authors of this work receive support from the Hilda and Preston Davis Foundation. The opinions and assertions expressed herein are those of the authors and are not to be construed as reflecting the views of the Davis Foundation.

Disclosure statement

All authors declare no conflict of interest.

Funding

This work was supported by the Hilda and Preston Davis Foundation [n/a].

ORCID

Erin E. Reilly http://orcid.org/0000-0001-9269-0747

References

Anderson, L. K., Murray, S. B., Ramirez, A. L., Rockwell, R., Le Grange, D., & Kaye, W. H. (2015). The integration of family-based treatment and dialectical behavior therapy for adolescent bulimia nervosa: Philosophical and practical considerations. *Eating Disorders*, *23*(4), 325–335. https://doi.org/10.1080/10640266.2015.1042319

Anestis, M. D., Peterson, C. B., Bardone-Cone, A. M., Klein, M. H., Mitchell, J. E., Crosby, R. D., Wonderlich, S. A., Crow, S. J., le Grange, D., & Joiner, T. E. (2009). Affective lability and impulsivity in a clinical sample of women with bulimia nervosa: The role of affect in severely dysregulated behavior. *International Journal of Eating Disorders*, *42*(3), 259–266. https://doi.org/10.1002/eat.20606

Arcelus, J., Mitchell, A. J., Wales, J., & Nielsen, S. (2011). Mortality rates in patients with anorexia nervosa and other eating disorders: A meta-analysis of 36 studies. *Archives of General Psychiatry*, *68*(7), 724–731. https://doi.org/10.1001/archgenpsychiatry.2011.74

Bankoff, S. M., Karpel, M. G., Forbes, H. E., & Pantalone, D. W. (2012). A systematic review of dialectical behavior therapy for the treatment of eating disorders. *Eating Disorders*, *20* (3), 196–215. https://doi.org/10.1080/10640266.2012.668478

Ben-Porath, D. D., Federici, A., Wisniewski, L., & Warren, M. (2014). Dialectical behavior therapy: Does it bring about improvements in affect regulation in individuals with eating disorders? *Journal of Contemporary Psychotherapy*, *44*(4), 245–251. https://doi.org/10.1007/s10879-014-9271-2

Berk, M. S., Starace, N. K., Black, V. P., & Avina, C. (2019). Implementation of dialectical behavior therapy with suicidal and self-harming adolescents in a community clinic. *Archives of Suicide Research*, 1–20. https://doi.org/10.1080/13811118.2018.1509750

Brown, T. A., Cusack, A., Anderson, L. K., Trim, J., Nakamura, T., Trunko, M. E., & Kaye, W. H. (2018). Efficacy of a partial hospital programme for adults with eating disorders. *European Eating Disorders Review*, *26*(3), 241–252.

Cook, N. E., & Gorraiz, M. (2016). Dialectical behavior therapy for nonsuicidal self-injury and depression among adolescents: Preliminary meta-analytic evidence. *Child and Adolescent Mental Health*, *21*(2), 81–89. https://doi.org/10.1111/camh.12112

Couturier, J., Kimber, M., & Szatmari, P. (2013). Efficacy of family-based treatment for adolescents with eating disorders: A systematic review and meta-analysis. *International Journal of Eating Disorders*, *46*(1), 3–11. https://doi.org/10.1002/eat.22042

Federici, A., & Wisniewski, L. (2012). Integrating dialectical behavior therapy and family-based treatment for multidiagnostic adolescent patients. In J. Alexander & J. Treasure (Eds.), *A collaborative approach to eating disorders* (pp. 177–188)). Routledge.

Fischer, S., & Grange, D. L. (2007). Comorbidity and high-risk behaviors in treatment-seeking adolescents with bulimia nervosa. *International Journal of Eating Disorders*, *40* (8), 751–753. https://doi.org/10.1002/eat.20442

Fischer, S., & Peterson, C. (2015). Dialectical behavior therapy for adolescent binge eating, purging, suicidal behavior, and non-suicidal self-injury: A pilot study. *Psychotherapy*, *52* (1), 78–92. https://doi.org/10.1037/a0036065

Groves, S., Backer, H. S., van den Bosch, W., & Miller, A. (2012). Dialectical behaviour therapy with adolescents. *Child and Adolescent Mental Health*, *17*(2), 65–75. https://doi.org/10.1111/j.1475-3588.2011.00611.x

Haynos, A. F., & Fruzzetti, A. E. (2011). Anorexia nervosa as a disorder of emotion dysregulation: Evidence and treatment implications. *Clinical Psychology: Science and Practice*, *18*(3), 183–202. https://doi.org/10.1111/j.1468-2850.2011.01250.x

Hill, D. M., Craighead, L. W., & Safer, D. L. (2011). Appetite-focused dialectical behavior therapy for the treatment of binge eating with purging: A preliminary trial. *International Journal of Eating Disorders*, *44*(3), 249–261. https://doi.org/10.1002/eat.20812

Johnston, J. A., O'Gara, J. S., Koman, S. L., Baker, C. W., & Anderson, D. A. (2015). A pilot study of Maudsley family therapy with group dialectical behavior therapy skills training in an intensive outpatient program for adolescent eating disorders. *Journal of Clinical Psychology*, *71*(6), 527–543. https://doi.org/10.1002/jclp.22176

Kazdin, A. E. (2007). Mediators and mechanisms of change in psychotherapy research. *Annual Review of Clinical Psychology*, *3*(1), 1–27. https://doi.org/10.1146/annurev.clinpsy.3.022806.091432

Klein, A. S., Skinner, J. B., & Hawley, K. M. (2013). Targeting binge eating through components of dialectical behavior therapy: Preliminary outcomes for individually supported diary card self-monitoring versus group-based DBT. *Psychotherapy*, *50*(4), 543–552. https://doi.org/10.1037/a0033130

Koerner, K., & Dimeff, L. A. (2007). Overview of dialectical behavior therapy. In L. A. Dimeff, & K. Koerner (Eds.), *Dialectical behavior therapy in clinical practice: Applications across disorders and settings; dialectical behavior therapy in clinical practice: Applications across disorders and settings* (pp. 1–18, Chapter xx, 363 Pages). New York, NY: Guilford Press.

Lavender, J. M., Wonderlich, S. A., Engel, S. G., Gordon, K. H., Kaye, W. H., & Mitchell, J. E. (2015). Dimensions of emotion dysregulation in anorexia nervosa and bulimia nervosa: A conceptual review of the empirical literature. *Clinical Psychology Review*, *40*, 111–122. https://doi.org/10.1016/j.cpr.2015.05.010

Le Grange, D., Crosby, R. D., Rathouz, P. J., & Leventhal, B. L. (2007). A randomized controlled comparison of family-based treatment and supportive psychotherapy for adolescent bulimia nervosa. *Archives of General Psychiatry*, *64*(9), 1049–1056. https://doi.org/10.1001/archpsyc.64.9.1049

Le Grange, D., Lock, J., Agras, W. S., Bryson, S. W., & Jo, B. (2015). Randomized clinical trial of family-based treatment and cognitive-behavioral therapy for adolescent bulimia nervosa. *Journal of the American Academy of Child & Adolescent Psychiatry*, *54*(11), 886–894. https://doi.org/10.1016/j.jaac.2015.08.008

Lenz, A. S., Taylor, R., Fleming, M., & Serman, N. (2014). Effectiveness of dialectical behavior therapy for treating eating disorders. *Journal of Counseling & Development*, *92*(1), 26–35. https://doi.org/10.1002/j.1556-6676.2014.00127.x

Linardon, J., Fairburn, C. G., Fitzsimmons-Craft, E. E., Wilfley, D. E., & Brennan, L. (2017). The empirical status of the third-wave behaviour therapies for the treatment of eating disorders: A systematic review. *Clinical Psychology Review*, *58*, 125–140. https://doi.org/10.1016/j.cpr.2017.10.005

Linehan, M. M. (1987). Dialectical behavior therapy: A cognitive behavioral approach to parasuicide. *Journal of Personality Disorders*, *1*(4), 328–333. https://doi.org/10.1521/pedi.1987.1.4.328

Linehan, M. M. (1991). Cognitive-behavioral treatment of chronically parasuicidal borderline patients. *Archives of General Psychiatry*, *48*(12), 1060–1064. https://doi.org/10.1001/archpsyc.1991.01810360024003

Linehan, M. M. (1993). *Cognitive-behavioral treatment of borderline personality disorder*. Guilford Publications.

Linehan, M. M., Kanter, J. W., & Comtois, K. A. (1999). Dialectical behavior therapy for borderline personality disorder: Efficacy, specificity, and cost effectiveness. In D. S. Janowsky (Ed.), *Psychotherapy indications and outcomes* (pp. 93–118). American Psychiatric Association.

Linehan, M. M., Comtois, K. A., Murray, A. M., Brown, M. Z., Gallop, R. J., Heard, H. L., Korslund, K. E., Tutek, D. A., Reynolds, S. K., & Lindenboim, N. (2006). Two-year randomized controlled trial and follow-up of dialectical behavior therapy vs therapy by experts for suicidal behaviors and borderline personality disorder. *Archives of General Psychiatry*, *63*(7), 757–766. https://doi.org/10.1001/archpsyc.63.7.757

Linehan, M. M., Korslund, K. E., Harned, M. S., Gallop, R. J., Lungu, A., Neacsiu, A. D., McDavid, J., Comtois, K. A., & Murray-Gregory, A. M. (2015). Dialectical behavior therapy for high suicide risk in individuals with borderline personality disorder: A randomized clinical trial and component analysis. *JAMA Psychiatry*, *72*(5), 475–482. https://doi.org/10.1001/jamapsychiatry.2014.3039

Lock, J., & Le Grange, D. (2013). *Treatment manual for anorexia nervos: A family-based approach*. New York, NY: Guilford Press.

Lock, J., Le Grange, D., Agras, W. S., & Dare, C. (2001). Treatment manual for anorexia nervosa. *A family-based approach*. NewYork/London: Guilford Press.

Lock, J., Le Grange, D., Agras, W. S., Moye, A., Bryson, S. W., & Jo, B. (2010). Randomized clinical trial comparing family-based treatment with adolescent-focused individual therapy for adolescents with anorexia nervosa. *Archives of General Psychiatry*, *67*(10), 1025–1032. https://doi.org/10.1001/archgenpsychiatry.2010.128

Lynch, T. R., Chapman, A. L., Rosenthal, M. Z., Kuo, J. R., & Linehan, M. M. (2006). Mechanisms of change in dialectical behavior therapy: Theoretical and empirical observations. *Journal of Clinical Psychology*, *62*(4), 459–480. https://doi.org/10.1002/jclp.20243

Lynch, T. R., Gray, K. L., Hempel, R. J., Titley, M., Chen, E. Y., & O'Mahen, H. A. (2013). Radically open-dialectical behavior therapy for adult anorexia nervosa: feasibility and outcomes from an inpatient program. *BMC Psychiatry*, *13*, 293.

MacPherson, H. A., Cheavens, J. S., & Fristad, M. A. (2013). Dialectical behavior therapy for adolescents: Theory, treatment adaptations, and empirical outcomes. *Clinical Child and Family Psychology Review*, *16*(1), 59–80. https://doi.org/10.1007/s10567-012-0126-7

Masson, P. C., von Ranson, K. M., Wallace, L. M., & Safer, D. L. (2013). A randomized wait-list controlled pilot study of dialectical behaviour therapy guided self-help for binge eating disorder. *Behaviour Research and Therapy*, *51*(11), 723–728. https://doi.org/10.1016/j.brat.2013.08.001

McCauley, E., Berk, M. S., Asarnow, J. R., Adrian, M., Cohen, J., Korslund, K., Avina, C., Hughes, J., Harned, M., Gallop, R., & Linehan, M. M. (2018). Efficacy of dialectical behavior therapy for adolescents at high risk for suicide: A randomized clinical trial. *JAMA Psychiatry*, *75*(8), 777–785. https://doi.org/10.1001/jamapsychiatry.2018.1109

Mehlum, L., Ramberg, M., Tørmoen, A. J., Haga, E., Diep, L. M., Stanley, B. H., Miller, A. L., Sund, A. M., & Grøholt, B. (2016). Dialectical behavior therapy compared with enhanced usual care for adolescents with repeated suicidal and self-harming behavior: Outcomes over a one-year follow-up. *Journal of the American Academy of Child & Adolescent Psychiatry*, *55*(4), 295–300. https://doi.org/10.1016/j.jaac.2016.01.005

Mehlum, L., Tørmoen, A. J., Ramberg, M., Haga, E., Diep, L. M., Laberg, S., Larsson, B. S., Stanley, B. H., Miller, A. L., Sund, A. M., & Grøholt, B. (2014). Dialectical behavior therapy for adolescents with repeated suicidal and self-harming behavior: A randomized trial. *Journal of the American Academy of Child & Adolescent Psychiatry*, *53*(10), 1082–1091. https://doi.org/10.1016/j.jaac.2014.07.003

Miller, A. L., Rathus, J. H., & Linehan, M. M. (2009). *Dialectical behavior therapy with suicidal adolescents*. New York, NY: Guilford Press.

Miller, A. L., Rathus, J. H., Linehan, M. M., Wetzler, S., & Leigh, E. (1997). Dialectical behavior therapy adapted for suicidal adolescents. *Journal of Psychiatric Practice®*, *3*(2), 78. https://doi.org/10.1097/00131746-199703000-00002

Mitchell, J. E., & Crow, S. (2006). Medical complications of anorexia nervosa and bulimia nervosa. *Current Opinion in Psychiatry*, *19*(4), 438–443. https://doi.org/10.1097/01.yco.0000228768.79097.3e

Murray, S. B., Anderson, L. K., Cusack, A., Nakamura, T., Rockwell, R., Griffiths, S., & Kaye, W. H. (2015). Integrating family-based treatment and dialectical behavior therapy for adolescent bulimia nervosa: Preliminary outcomes of an open pilot trial. *Eating Disorders*, *23*(4), 336–344. https://doi.org/10.1080/10640266.2015.1044345

Navarro-Haro, M. V., Botella, C., Guillen, V., Moliner, R., Marco, H., Jorquera, M., ... Garcia-Palacios, A. (2018). Dialectical behavior therapy in the treatment of borderline personality disorder and eating disorders comorbidity: A pilot study in a naturalistic setting. *Cognitive Therapy and Research*, 1–14. https://doi.org/10.1007/s10608-018-9906-9

Neacsiu, A. D., Rizvi, S. L., & Linehan, M. M. (2010). Dialectical behavior therapy skills use as a mediator and outcome of treatment for borderline personality disorder. *Behaviour Research and Therapy*, *48*(9), 832–839. https://doi.org/10.1016/j.brat.2010.05.017

Palmer, R.L., Birchall, H., Damani, S., Gatward, N., McGrain, L., & Parker, L. (2003). A dialectical behavior therapy program for people with an eating disorder and borderline personality disorder–description and outcome. *International Journal of Eating Disorders*, *33*(3), 281–286.

Peebles, R., Wilson, J. L., & Lock, J. D. (2011). Self-injury in adolescents with eating disorders: Correlates and provider bias. *Journal of Adolescent Health*, *48*(3), 310–313. https://doi.org/10.1016/j.jadohealth.2010.06.017

Pennell, A., Webb, C., Agar, P., Federici, A., & Couturier, J. (2019). Implementation of dialectical behavior therapy in a day hospital setting for adolescents with eating disorders. *Journal of the Canadian Academy of Child and Adolescent Psychiatry*, *28*(1), 21–29. Retrieved from https://www.ncbi.nlm.nih.gov/pmc/articles/PMC6457442/

Perepletchikova, F., Axelrod, S. R., Kaufman, J., Rounsaville, B. J., Douglas-Palumberi, H., & Miller, A. L. (2011). Adapting dialectical behaviour therapy for children: Towards a new research agenda for paediatric suicidal and non-suicidal self-injurious behaviours. *Child and Adolescent Mental Health*, *16*(2), 116–121. https://doi.org/10.1111/j.1475-3588.2010.00583.x

Perepletchikova, F., Nathanson, D., Axelrod, S. R., Merrill, C., Walker, A., Grossman, M., Mauer, E., Kaufman, J., Flye, B., Mauer, E., Walkup, J., & Rebeta, J. (2017). Randomized clinical trial of dialectical behavior therapy for preadolescent children with disruptive mood dysregulation disorder: Feasibility and outcomes. *Journal of the American Academy of Child & Adolescent Psychiatry*, *56*, 832–840. https://doi.org/10.1016/j.jaac.2017.07.789

Peterson, C. M., Van Diest, A. M. K., Mara, C. A., & Matthews, A. (2019). Dialectical behavioral therapy skills group as an adjunct to family-based therapy in adolescents with restrictive eating disorders. *Eating Disorders*, *28*(1)1–13. https://doi.org/10.1080/10640266.2019.1568101

Rahmani, M., Omidi, A., Asemi, Z., & Akbari, H. (2018). The effect of dialectical behaviour therapy on binge eating, difficulties in emotion regulation and bmi in overweight patients with binge-eating disorder. *A Randomized Controlled Trial, Mental Health & Prevention*, *9*, 13–18.

Rathus, J., & Miller, A. L. (2015). *DBT skills manual for adolescents*. New York, NY: Guilford Press.

Rathus, J. H., & Miller, A. L. (2002). Dialectical behavior therapy adapted for suicidal adolescents. *Suicide and Life-Threatening Behavior*, *32*(2), 146–157. https://doi.org/10.1521/suli.32.2.146.24399

Rienecke, R. D., Accurso, E. C., Lock, J., & Le Grange, D. (2016). Expressed emotion, family functioning, and treatment outcome for adolescents with anorexia nervosa. *European Eating Disorders Review*, *24*(1), 43–51. https://doi.org/10.1002/erv.2389

Rienecke, R. D., Lebow, J., Lock, J., & Le Grange, D. (2017). Family profiles of expressed emotion in adolescent patients with anorexia nervosa and their parents. *Journal of Clinical Child & Adolescent Psychology*, *46*(3), 428–436. https://doi.org/10.1080/15374416.2015.1030755

Safer, D. L., Couturier, J. L., & Lock, J. (2007). Dialectical behavior therapy modified for adolescent binge eating disorder: A case report. *Cognitive and Behavioral Practice*, *14*(2), 157–167. https://doi.org/10.1016/j.cbpra.2006.06.001

Safer, D. L., & Jo, B. (2010). Outcome from a randomized controlled trial of group therapy for binge eating disorder: Comparing dialectical behavior therapy adapted for binge eating to an active comparison group therapy. *Behavior Therapy, 41*(1), 106–120. https://doi.org/10.1016/j.beth.2009.01.006

Sahin, Z., Vinnars, B., Gorman, B. S., Wilczek, A., Åsberg, M., & Barber, J. P. (2018). Clinical severity as a moderator of outcome in psychodynamic and dialectical behavior therapies for borderline personality disorder. *Personality Disorders: Theory, Research, and Treatment, 9*(5), 437–446. https://doi.org/10.1037/per0000276

Sakaluk, J. K., Williams, A., Kilshaw, R., & Rhyner, K. T. (2019). Evaluating the evidential value of empirically supported psychological treatments (ESTs): A meta-scientific review. *Journal of Abnormal Psychology*. https://psyarxiv.com/pzbhw/download/?format=pdf

Salbach, H., Klinkowski, N., Pfeiffer, E., Lehmkuhl, U., & Korte, A. (2007). *Dialectical Behavior Therapy for Adolescents with Anorexia and Bulimia Nervosa (Dbt-an/ Bn)— a Pilot Study [Dialektisch Behaviorale Therapie Für Jugendliche Patientinnen Mit Anorexia Und Bulimia Nervosa (Dbt-an/bn)—eine Pilotstudie] Praxis Der Kinderpsychologie Und Kinderpsychiatrie, 56*, 91–108.

Salbach-Andrae, H., Bohnekamp, I., Pfeiffer, E., Lehmkuhl, U., & Miller, A. L. (2008). Dialectical behavior therapy of anorexia and bulimia nervosa among adolescents: A case series. *Cognitive and Behavioral Practice, 15*(4), 415–425. https://doi.org/10.1016/j.cbpra.2008.04.001

Sim, L., Adrian, M., Zeman, J., Cassano, M., & Friedrich, W. N. (2009). Adolescent deliberate self-harm: Linkages to emotion regulation and family emotional climate. *Journal of Research on Adolescence, 19*(1), 75–91. https://doi.org/10.1111/j.1532-7795.2009.00582.x

Striegel-Moore, R. H., Leslie, D., Petrill, S. A., Garvin, V., & Rosenheck, R. A. (2000). One-year use and cost of inpatient and outpatient services among female and male patients with an eating disorder: Evidence from a national database of health insurance claims. *International Journal of Eating Disorders, 27*(4), 381–389. https://doi.org/10.1002/(SICI)1098-108X(200005)27:4<381::AID-EAT2>3.0.CO;2-U

Tackett, J. L., Lilienfeld, S. O., Patrick, C. J., Johnson, S. L., Krueger, R. F., Miller, J. D., Oltmanns, T. F., & Shrout, P. E. (2017). It's time to broaden the replicability conversation: Thoughts for and from clinical psychological science. *Perspectives on Psychological Science, 12*(5), 742–756. https://doi.org/10.1177/1745691617690042

Telch, C. F., Agras, W. S., & Linehan, M. M. (2000). Group dialectical behavior therapy for binge-eating disorder: A preliminary, uncontrolled trial. *Behavior Therapy, 31*(3), 569–582. https://doi.org/10.1016/S0005-7894(00)80031-3

Telch, C. F., Agras, W. S., & Linehan, M. M. (2001). Dialectical behavior therapy for binge eating disorder. *Journal of Consulting and Clinical Psychology, 69*(6), 1061–1065. https://doi.org/10.1037/0022-006X.69.6.1061

Treasure, J., & Russell, G. (2011). The case for early intervention in anorexia nervosa: Theoretical exploration of maintaining factors. *The British Journal of Psychiatry, 199*(1), 5–7.

Waxman, S. E. (2009). A systematic review of impulsivity in eating disorders. *European Eating Disorders Review, 17*(6), 408–425. https://doi.org/10.1002/erv.952

Wilkinson, P. O. (2018). Dialectical behavior therapy—A highly effective treatment for some adolescents who self-harm. *JAMA Psychiatry, 75*(8), 786–787. https://doi.org/10.1001/jamapsychiatry.2018.1079

Zabala, M. J., Macdonald, P., & Treasure, J. (2009). Appraisal of caregiving burden, expressed emotion and psychological distress in families of people with eating disorders: A systematic review. *European Eating Disorders Review: The Professional Journal of the Eating Disorders Association, 17*(5), 338–349. https://doi.org/10.1002/erv.925

Zapolski, T. C., & Smith, G. T. (2017). Pilot study: Implementing a brief DBT skills program in schools to reduce health risk behaviors among early adolescents. *The Journal of School Nursing, 33*(3), 198–204. https://doi.org/10.1177/1059840516673188

Correlates of co-occurring eating disorders and substance use disorders: a case for dialectical behavior therapy

Kimberly Claudat, Tiffany A. Brown, Leslie K. Anderson, Gina Bongiorno, Laura A. Berner, Erin Reilly, Tana Luo, Natalia C. Orloff, and Walter H. Kaye

ABSTRACT

Given the high rates of comorbidity between eating disorders (EDs) and substance use disorders (SUDs), it is important to develop effective treatment approaches for individuals with both an ED and SUD (ED-SUD). To date, there is limited information guiding the concurrent treatment of these disorders. To build on existing research, the present study compared adult patients with ED-SUD ($n = 36$) to patients with ED-only ($n = 62$) in terms of demographics, psychiatric comorbidity, and self-reported eating disorder and related psychopathology. Results indicated that ED-SUD patients had a higher number of psychiatric comorbidities, were more likely to be prescribed mood stabilizers, and were more sensitive to reward. They also reported greater difficulty with emotion regulation, including more difficulty engaging in goal-directed activity, higher impulsivity, and more limited access to emotion regulation strategies. These differences highlight the importance of targeting emotion dysregulation for ED-SUD, and provide evidence for the importance of integrated, transdiagnostic treatment to simultaneously address the SUD, ED, and other psychiatric comorbidities. Implications for tailoring treatment are discussed with a focus on Dialectical Behavior Therapy (DBT).

Clinical implications

- Compared to patients with only an eating disorder, those with both an eating disorder and substance use disorder had a higher number of psychiatric comorbidities, were more likely to be prescribed mood stabilizers, and were more sensitive to reward.
- Eating disorder and substance use disorder patients also reported greater difficulty with emotion regulation, including more difficulty engaging in goal directed activity, higher impulsivity, and more limited access to emotion regulation strategies.

- These findings highlight the importance of targeting emotion dysregulation for ED-SUD, and provide evidence for the importance of addressing substance use, eating behaviors, and other psychiatric comorbidities with an integrated, transdiagnostic treatment approach such as Dialectical Behavior Therapy.

Substance use disorders (SUDs) and eating disorders (EDs) commonly co-occur (CASA, 2003). Indeed, a recent meta-analysis indicated that among those with ED, the lifetime prevalence rate of a comorbid SUD was 21.9% (Bahji et al., 2019). Tobacco, caffeine, and alcohol are reported as the most prevalent SUDs for individuals with EDs (Bahji et al., 2019). Sedatives, cannabis, stimulants, and over-the-counter products such as laxatives, diuretics, and diet pills are also commonly abused (Fouladi et al., 2015; Roerig et al., 2003; Steffen et al., 2007). Research suggests that ED patients with co-occurring SUDs experience lower rates of treatment response, higher relapse rates, more severe medical complications, greater impairment, poorer long-term outcome, and are at higher risk of early mortality (Glasner-Edwards et al., 2011; Harrop & Marlatt, 2010; Keel et al., 1999; Lindblad et al., 2016).

Given the high-risk nature of individuals with co-occurring EDs and SUDs (ED-SUD), and poor outcomes associated with their treatment, it is important to identify whether effective treatment interventions for this population. A major barrier to identifying treatment targets for ED-SUD is the paucity of research comprehensively characterizing the treatment-seeking ED-SUD patient population. Below, we outline the existing literature characterizing ED-SUD and associated features.

Severity of illness and psychiatric comorbidity

Separately, EDs and SUDs have the highest and second-highest mortality rates of all psychological disorders (Harris & Barraclough, 1998; Preti et al., 2009). Both EDs and SUDs often present with comorbid mood disorders, anxiety disorders, posttraumatic stress disorder (PTSD), and borderline personality disorder (BPD; Blinder et al., 2006; Compton et al., 2007; Courbasson et al., 2005; Pennay et al., 2011). Becker and Grilo (2015) found that among patients with binge eating disorder (BED), those with both mood and substance use disorders had the most severe ED symptoms, and higher rates of personality disorders. In a retrospective chart review, Kirkpatrick et al. (2019) found that for adolescents with ED, those with comorbid SUD had higher rates of self-harm and purging, and had a higher BMI at intake. Finally, a small study of an inpatient sample showed that those with ED-SUD were more likely to be diagnosed with a Cluster B personality disorder compared with those with ED alone (Grilo et al., 1995).

ED Diagnosis. Several studies have investigated whether co-occurring SUD is more common in anorexia nervosa-restricting type (AN-R), anorexia nervosa-binge-purge type (AN-BP), or bulimia nervosa (BN). Theoretically, it is believed that binge-purge behaviors are more closely linked to substance abuse, as there is evidence for an increased association between these behaviors and impulsivity and emotion regulation difficulties (e.g., Kober, 2014; Lavender et al., 2015). One large study found that within ED patients, BN, and AN-BP patients had the highest prevalence of comorbid substance use, whereas AN-R participants generally had the lowest (Krug et al., 2009). Root et al. (2010) found that across eating disorder groups, the BN and AN-BP groups were more likely to report alcohol abuse and diet pill use relative to the AN group, and the AN-BP group was more likely than the AN-R group to have alcohol abuse, use diet pills, stimulants, and engage in polysubstance abuse. Along the same lines, Fouladi et al. (2015) found patients with BN used substances with higher frequencies compared to patients with AN-R, BED, and EDNOS, and those with AN-BP were more likely to use substances than those with AN-R. Moreover, higher frequencies of binge eating and purging were associated with higher frequencies of substance use. Finally, a meta-analysis on this topic by Bahji et al. (2019) revealed that prevalence rates of SUD were significantly higher among individuals with binge-purge behaviors than those with only restrictive behaviors.

Temperament and emotion dysregulation

Temperament (reward sensitivity, impulsivity, novelty seeking) and underlying emotion regulation difficulties serve as common risk and maintenance factors for EDs and SUDs. Recent research provides compelling support for theories of emotion regulation to explain the co-occurrence of disordered eating and substance abuse (e.g., Dir et al., 2013). Specifically, these theories posit that individuals engage in these maladaptive coping strategies to alleviate negative affect (Anestis et al., 2009). In support of this, existing findings indicate that affective instability, impulsivity, negative urgency, and novelty seeking are common in individuals with EDs who engage in substance abuse (e.g., Dawe & Loxton, 2004; Fischer et al., 2012). For example, a study investigating temperament found that binge eating was associated with increased impulsivity and risky decision-making (Mobbs et al., 2011). Similarly, in a study of undergraduate men and women, researchers found that negative urgency, a component of emotion dysregulation that includes the tendency to act rashly when distressed, was significantly associated with problematic alcohol use and disordered eating (Dir et al., 2013). Finally, Loxton and Dawe (2001) found that adolescent girls who abused alcohol and engaged in disordered eating were more sensitive to reward than adolescent girls who did not engage in any of these behaviors.

Overall, extant literature highlights the complex nature of ED-SUD presentations. Thus, traditional treatment programs have targeted EDs and SUDs sequentially. However, interest in integrated treatment approaches has grown (Dennis et al., 2014), and research indicates that patients who do not receive integrated treatment have poorer treatment outcomes (e.g., Drake et al., 2001). Nevertheless, there is limited research on what such an integrated approach should optimally target, and there is no consensus in the field about the best treatment modality for the ED-SUD population.

One potentially promising intervention for ED-SUD is Dialectical Behavior Therapy (DBT), which is a treatment based on an emotion regulation model (Neacsiu et al., 2014). In DBT, psychoeducation on this model is provided, and patients are encouraged to accept and learn to tolerate their emotional experiences, while also learning alternative methods of coping with their emotions. DBT is a well-established treatment for individuals with multiple and severe psychological disorders (Linehan, 1993), and has been adapted for use with EDs (Safer et al., 2001; Telch et al., 2001). Its further adaptation and testing for individuals with co-occurring SUDs and BPD (Dimeff & Linehan, 2008) support its use to target multiple problem areas in an integrated manner. Only one study has investigated the application of DBT for co-occurring EDs and substance use. Findings from this study are promising, suggesting that integrated DBT for ED-SUD treatment is associated with decreased substance use severity and frequency, decreased emotional eating, and increased levels of confidence in ability to resist urges for substance use (Courbasson et al., 2012). Given the limited research on DBT for ED-SUD, a better understanding of factors associated with ED-SUD compared to ED or SUD alone may be helpful in identifying potential treatment targets to address both disorders simultaneously.

The impetus for the current study was to add to this limited literature by reproducing previous research findings in a treatment-seeking ED population and discussing how these empirical findings can guide treatment recommendations for ED-SUD. Consequently, the present study examined differences between patients with EDs only to patients with ED-SUD on demographics, psychiatric comorbidity, and self-reported eating disorder and related psychopathology. Given previous research findings, we hypothesized that individuals with ED-SUD would be more likely than ED only to engage in binge eating/purging, and to have a bulimic-spectrum eating disorder, BPD symptoms, higher rates of psychiatric comorbidities, self-harm, and suicidality, greater difficulties with emotion regulation, and more reward sensitivity.

Methods

Participants & procedures

Participants were 98 adult patients admitted to a partial hospital program for EDs between August 2016 and November 2018. Participants completed clinical interviews and survey measures within 14 days of treatment admission. Eating disorder and comorbidities were diagnosed using either the Mini Neuropsychiatric Interview (MINI; Sheehan et al., 1998) or the Structured

Clinical Interview for DSM-5 Disorder (SCID-5; First et al., 2015) administered by trained, bachelor's-level research assistants. Suicidality risk was assessed using the MINI suicidality module. Thirty-six patients were diagnosed with a SUD. Of those, 19.4% were diagnosed with an alcohol use disorder (n = 19) and 25.5% were diagnosed with a non-alcohol SUD (n = 25). Of the 25 patients with a non-alcohol SUD, 20% had a sedative-hypnotic-anxiolytic use disorder (n = 5), 52% had a cannabis use disorder (n = 13), 20% had a stimulant use disorder (n = 5), 8% had an opioid use disorder (n = 2), and 4% had a hallucinogen use disorder (n = 4).

Measures

Eating Disorder Symptoms were assessed using the Eating Disorder Examination–Questionnaire (EDE-Q; Fairburn & Beglin, 1994). The Global score was used to assess eating disorder symptoms during the previous 28 days. Internal consistency for the EDE-Q Global score in the present study was excellent (α =.96).

Trait Anxiety was assessed using the self-report State-Trait Anxiety Inventory—Trait Subscale (STAI-T; Spielberger et al., 1970). Items (e.g., "I feel pleasant") are rated on a 4-point scale reflecting how often participants generally feel, and are scored so that higher scores reflect higher anxiety. Internal consistency for the STAI-T subscale was α = .90.

Depressive symptoms were assessed using the Beck Depression Inventory (BDI-II; Beck et al., 1996). The BDI-II includes 21-item self-report items to evaluate the severity of depressive symptoms on a 4-point scale, with higher scores indicating greater depression. Internal consistency within the present sample was excellent (α = .93).

Emotion Regulation Difficulties were assessed using the Difficulties in Emotion Regulation Scale (DERS; Gratz & Roemer, 2004). The DERS is a 36-item self-report questionnaire that includes six subscales: Nonacceptance of Emotional Responses (Nonacceptance), Difficulties Engaging in Goal-Directed Behaviors (Goals), Impulse Control Difficulties (Impulse), Lack of Emotional Awareness (Awareness), Limited Access to Emotion Regulation Strategies (Strategies), and Lack of Emotional Clarity (Clarity). Items (e.g., "I experience my emotions as overwhelming and out of control") are rated on a 5-point scale (1 = almost never to 5 = almost always). The internal consistency of the DERS and its subscales ranged from good to excellent in the present sample (Total α = .95, Nonacceptance α = .91, Goals α = .89, Impulse α = .89, Awareness α = .86, Strategies α = .91, Clarity α = .85).

Sensitivity to Punishment/Reward was assessed using the Sensitivity to Punishment and Sensitivity to Reward Questionnaire (SPSRQ; Torrubia et al., 2001). The SPSRQ includes 44 items assessing sensitivity to punishment (e.g., "Are you often afraid of new or unexpected situations?") and reward (e.g., "Does the good prospect of obtaining money motivate you strongly to do some things?") and has demonstrated strong psychometric properties (Torrubia et al., 2001). Internal consistency within the present sample was excellent for the reward ($\alpha = .82$) and punishment subscales ($\alpha = .88$)

Borderline Personality Disorder Symptoms were assessed using the Borderline Evaluation of Severity over Time (BEST; Pfohl et al., 2009). BEST is a 15-item, self-report the measure of past-month BPD symptom severity and has demonstrated adequate psychometric properties (Pfohl et al., 2009). Items (e.g., "feelings of emptiness") are rated on a 5-point scale based on the level of distress/impairment (1 = none/slight to 5 = extreme). Internal consistency in the present sample was acceptable ($\alpha = .76$).

Data analyses

Participants with ED only and ED-SUD were compared on demographic variables, comorbidities, psychotropic medications, and self-report measures at treatment admission. Categorical variables were compared using chi-square analyses and continuous variables were compared using one-way analyses of variance. To control for multiple comparisons, the threshold for significance was set at $p = .01$. Values below the threshold of $p < .05$ are discussed as trends, given the exploratory nature of the analyses and limited data on this topic to date.

Results

Table 1 presents demographic differences between ED and ED-SUD patients. There were no significant differences in age, BMI, length of illness, history of previous treatment, gender, ethnicity, diagnosis, or engagement in purging behaviors between groups, and only trend-level differences in racial background and the likelihood of engaging in objective binge eating episodes.

Table 2 presents differences in comorbidity and psychotropic medication use at admission between ED and ED-SUD patients. ED-SUD patients had a significantly greater number of psychiatric comorbidities and were more likely to be taking a mood stabilizer at treatment admission compared to ED patients. There was a trend towards ED-SUD patients being more likely to be diagnosed with panic disorder and posttraumatic stress disorder compared to ED patients.

Table 3 presents the differences between ED and ED-SUD patients on self-reported measures of eating disorder and related psychopathology. ED-SUD patients had higher scores on multiple subscales of the DERS—DERS Goals, DERS Impulse, and DERS Strategies—compared to ED patients. Additionally, ED-SUD patients reported significantly greater SPSRQ-Reward scores than those without a SUD. There was a trend towards individuals with a SUD reporting greater STAI-Trait, DERS Total, and SPSRQ-Punishment scores.

Table 1. Comparing patients with and without alcohol or substance use disorders on demographics.

Variable	SUD (n = 36) M(SD)/n(%)	No SUD (n = 62) M(SD)/n(%)	F/x	p
Age	25.49 (6.63)	24.082 (6.21)	1.12	.29
Admit BMI	20.78 (3.33)	21.01 (5.13)	0.06	.81
Length of Illness	10.88 (7.00)	9.25 (7.93)	1.02	.32
Previous ED treatment	20 (55.6)	43 (69.4)	1.89	.17
Gender			0.95	.62
Female	30 (83.3)	55 (90.2)		
Male	5 (13.9)	5 (8.2)		
Genderqueer/Non-conforming/Non-binary	1 (2.8)	1 (1.6)		
Race			10.91	.03
Caucasian	31 (86.1)	50 (83.3)		
Asian	3 (8.3)	3 (5.0)		
African American	0 (0.0)	2 (3.3)		
Native American/Alaskan Native	2 (5.6)	0 (0.0)		
Other	0 (0.0)	5 (8.3)		
Ethnicity			2.14	.14
Hispanic	2 (5.6)	11 (18.3)		
Non-Hispanic	34 (94.4)	49 (81.6)		
Diagnosis			5.38	.25
Anorexia Nervosa—Restricting	11 (30.6)	22 (35.5)		
Anorexia Nervosa—Binge/Purge	4 (11.1)	8 (12.9)		
Bulimia Nervosa	13 (36.1)	10 (16.1)		
Avoidant Restrictive Food Intake Disorder	1 (2.8)	2 (3.2)		
Other Specified Feeding or Eating Disorder	7 (19.4)	20 (32.3)		
Eating Disorder Behaviors Endorsed				
Objective Binge Episodes	18 (50.0)	17 (27.4)	5.06	.03
Purging	19 (52.8)	30 (48.4)	0.18	.68

Note. SUD = Alcohol or Substance Use Disorder; BMI = Body Mass Index

Discussion

The present study sought to describe differences between ED patients with and without a SUD at treatment admission. Results demonstrated that ED-SUD patients reported a greater number of comorbid psychiatric diagnoses and were more likely to be prescribed mood stabilizers. They also reported greater difficulty engaging in goal-directed activity, higher impulsivity, more limited access to emotion regulation strategies, and higher reward sensitivity. There were trend-level differences suggesting that individuals with ED-SUD were more likely to engage in objective binge episodes, be diagnosed with panic disorder and posttraumatic stress disorder, and to report higher trait anxiety, global emotion dysregulation, and sensitivity to punishment.

Results are largely consistent with our hypotheses and previous research demonstrating higher rates of psychiatric comorbidity (Compton et al., 2007), emotion regulation difficulties, and reward sensitivity (Loxton & Dawe, 2001) in ED-SUD samples. Partially consistent with previous research (e.g., Bahji et al., 2019), our results suggested a trend towards a higher frequency of binge eating

Table 2. Comparing patients with and without alcohol or substance use disorders on comorbidity.

Variable	SUD (n = 36*) M(SD)/n(%)	No SUD (n = 62) M(SD)/n(%)	F/x	p
Comorbid Diagnoses				
Number of Comorbidities	**2.56 (1.70)**	**1.52 (1.36)**	**11.02**	**.001**
Major Depressive Disorder, Current	21 (58.3)	24 (38.7)	3.53	.06
Bipolar Disorder I or II, Current	3 (8.3)	2 (3.2)	1.23	.27
Panic Disorder, Current	11 (30.6)	7 (11.3)	5.64	.02
Agoraphobia, Current	5 (13.9)	4 (6.5)	1.51	.22
Social Anxiety Disorder, Current	13 (36.1)	16 (25.8)	1.16	.28
Specific Phobia, Current	1 (2.8)	2 (3.2)	0.02	.90
Generalized Anxiety Disorder, Current	17 (47.2)	22 (35.5)	1.31	.25
Obsessive Compulsive Disorder, Current	9 (25.0)	7 (11.3)	3.38	.07
Posttraumatic Stress Disorder, Current	12 (33.3)	8 (12.9)	5.85	.02
Alcohol Use Disorder, Current	19 (52.8)	–		
Substance Use Disorder, Current	25 (69.4)	–		
Suicidality/Self-Harm				
Suicidality Risk			6.76	.08
Low	6 (16.7)	11 (17.7)		
Moderate	2 (5.6)	8 (12.9)		
High	20 (55.6)	19 (30.6)		
Past Suicide Attempt	7 (19.4)	13 (21.0)	0.03	.86
Current Self-Harm	2 (5.6)	3 (4.8)	0.02	.88
Medication at Admission				
Antidepressant Medication	20 (60.0)	38 (70.3)	0.88	.35
Atypical Antipsychotics	11 (33.3)	10 (18.5)	2.46	.12
Mood Stabilizer	**16 (48.5)**	**12 (22.2)**	**6.47**	**.01**

Note. SUD = Alcohol or Substance Use Disorder; Diagnoses were assessed using the Mini Neuropsychiatric Interview (MINI) or the Structured Clinical Interview for DSM-5 Disorders. Suicidality risk and self-harm were assessed using the MINI. *Due to missing data, participants ranged from n = 33–36 for the SUD group and n = 54–62 for the non-SUD group. Bolded values represent significant differences at p <.01.

in ED-SUD, although there were no differences between ED and ED-SUD groups on purging. Furthermore, patients with bulimic syndromes were not significantly more likely to have a SUD. While this is somewhat inconsistent with previous research (Krug et al., 2009; Root et al., 2010), results support examining substance use across ED diagnoses. In contrast, with previous research, we did not find evidence for higher levels of self-harm or BPD symptoms in the ED-SUD group. Previous research supporting increased self-harm in ED-SUD has been in adolescent samples (Kirkpatrick et al., 2019), which may also explain this discrepancy. While previous research has found higher cluster B symptoms in ED-SUD (Grilo et al., 1995), the lack of significant differences between ED and ED-SUD in our sample may be due to the relatively high scores on the BEST in both groups. Indeed, both groups scored similarly to patient samples with BPD (Pfohl et al., 2009).

Table 3. Comparing patients with and without alcohol and substance use disorders on self-report measures of eating disorder and related psychopathology.

	SUD (n = 36)	No SUD (n = 62)			
Variable	M(SD)/n(%)	M(SD)/n(%)	F/x	p	d
EDE-Q Global Score	4.29 (1.22)	3.92 (1.55)	1.47	.23	.27
STAI-Trait	64.34 (9.31)	59.03 (10.75)	5.99	.02	.53
BDI-II	36.89 (11.02)	32.26 (13.42)	3.08	.08	.38
DERS Total	132.38 (24.08)	119.11 (27.43)	5.79	.02	.51
DERS Nonacceptance	21.83 (5.54)	20.56 (6.61)	0.95	.33	.21
DERS Goals	**20.36 (3.94)**	**17.85 (5.03)**	**6.58**	**.01**	**.56**
DERS Impulse	**21.39 (5.74)**	**17.11 (6.73)**	**10.16**	**.002**	**.68**
DERS Strategies	**30.08 (6.89)**	**25.81 (8.21)**	**6.89**	**.01**	**.56**
DERS Awareness	21.67 (5.60)	21.41 (4.91)	0.10	.81	.05
DERS Clarity	17.06 (4.56)	16.36 (4.55)	0.53	.47	.15
SPSRQ Punishment	18.50 (3.42)	15.50 (5.52)	4.41	.04	.65
SPSRQ Reward	**15.17 (5.16)**	**10.87 (3.84)**	**11.56**	**.001**	**.95**
BEST	38.63 (10.41)	33.63 (10.65)	2.50	.12	.47

SUD = Alcohol or Substance Use Disorder; EDE-Q = Eating Disorder Examination—Questionnaire; STAI—Trait = State-Trait Anxiety Inventory, Trait Subscale; BDI-II = Beck Depression Inventory—II; DERS Total = Difficulties in Emotion Regulation Scale; Nonacceptance = DERS Nonacceptance of Emotional Responses; Goals = DERS Difficulties Engaging in Goal-Directed Behavior; Impulse = DERS Impulse Control Difficulties; Strategies = DERS Limited Access to Emotion Regulation Strategies; Awareness = DERS Lack of Emotional Awareness; Clarity = DERS Lack of Emotional Clarity; SPSRQ = Sensitivity to Punishment/ Sensitivity to Reward Scale; BEST = Borderline Symptoms over Time. *Due to missing data, participants ranged from n = 15–36 for the SUD group and n = 24–64 for the non-SUD group. Bolded values represent significant differences at $p < .01$.

Clinical implications

Taken together with previous research, several of these findings have important implications for developing a treatment approach for the ED-SUD population, and provide a rationale for the usefulness of DBT to target these disorders concurrently.

Psychiatric comorbidity

Overall, results demonstrating a greater number of comorbid diagnoses for the ED-SUD group support the need for integrated treatment, which is consistent with recent calls from experts within the field (Dennis et al., 2014). DBT takes a behavioral approach, treating behaviors, regardless of their diagnostic association, according to a specific hierarchy. Given the complexity of ED-SUD cases and the tendency for these patients to vacillate between ED and substance use behaviors over time (Dennis & Helfman, 2010), an integrated, transdiagnostic approach may be useful in treating both behavioral presentations. Importantly, we did not find evidence for ED diagnostic differences between ED-SUD and ED only groups, lending further support for a transdiagnostic approach to ED-SUD treatment.

DBT provides a comprehensive framework for effectively working with the multiple comorbidities observed in ED-SUD patients. In particular, the focus on the DBT hierarchy may help address vacillation between ED-SUD and other comorbid symptoms. The DBT hierarchy systematically addresses the most severe and life-threatening symptoms first, to help avoid shifting treatment targets throughout treatment. Additionally, skills generalization may be particularly important in this population. Phone coaching, which is a part of DBT, may be useful in helping patients to generalize skills to multiple behaviors across environments.

Regarding specific disorders, the non-statistically significant elevation in the likelihood of PTSD in the ED-SUD group compared to the ED alone group suggests that trauma symptoms may be a relevant treatment target for ED patients generally. Indeed, groups are working to develop protocols for the concurrent treatment of ED and PTSD (e.g., Trottier & MacDonald, 2017), while existing trauma protocols are commonly used to treat PTSD in these populations such as the DBT/Prolonged Exposure protocol (Harned et al., 2012).

Heightened emotion dysregulation

Our study shows that ED-SUD patients report significantly greater difficulties with emotion regulation. More specifically, ED-SUD patients in our sample endorsed difficulties with regulating behavior when distressed, engaging in goal-directed behavior when distressed, and accessing strategies for feeling better when distressed. Moreover, ED-SUD patients were more likely to already be prescribed a mood stabilizer; thus, despite previous treatment for emotion dysregulation they continued to have difficulty in this area. This is consistent with our hypothesis and points to emotion regulation as a critical treatment target. As previously discussed, DBT was specifically developed to provide education on emotion dysregulation and provide individuals with adaptive emotion regulation skills. Several skills were added to the DBT for SUD model to specifically address the heightened impulsivity reported by ED-SUD patients. These skills include Burning Bridges to persons, places, and things associated with substance abuse and Adaptive Denial of urges for substance use.

Reward sensitivity and punishment

The present findings that patients with ED-SUD report higher reward sensitivity to highlight the importance of assessing for and addressing temperament in this treatment population. Reward sensitivity may be an underlying mechanism that drives an individual's substance use and ED behaviors. For instance, substance use and ED behaviors may be highly rewarding in the moment; hence, patients seek the short-term rewards of addictive behaviors despite their long-term, negative consequences. Furthermore, a potential obstacle to abstinence from ED behaviors and substances of abuse is the non-rewarding aspect of abstinence (e.g., physiological discomfort associated with withdrawal, increased emotional discomfort, finding activities less enjoyable). Several skills taught in DBT for SUDs target these barriers. Contingency management strategies to reduce cues and access to substances and behaviors (e.g., Burning Bridges), as well as reinforcement of adaptive behavior, are essential to treatment. Specifically, Community Reinforcement (e.g., mindfully observing positives in relationships when abstinent, generally seeking environments that support and reinforce abstinence), and Abstinence Sampling (committing to shorter periods of sobriety to reach rewarding milestones) focus on the reinforcement of healthy behaviors.

In conjunction with findings on reward sensitivity, the trend towards the significance of increased punishment sensitivity in this ED-SUD population suggests that for some patients, holding patients accountable to treatment goals and implementing consequences and rewards accordingly may be important for behavior change. For example, using behavioral contracts and administering drug analysis screens to monitor substance use may be helpful. The DBT skill of Pros and Cons may help patients to identifying negative consequences of substance use.

Strengths and limitations

The present study has several strengths, including the use of structured clinical interviews to assess diagnoses and an examination of a broad range of constructs theoretically relevant to eating and substance use disorders. As such, this study adds to the limited literature investigating factors characterizing the ED-SUD population. However, there are several limitations worth noting. First, participants were drawn from a treatment-seeking sample presenting at a higher level of care. As such, results may not be representative of individuals with ED-SUD in the broader community. The modest ED-SUD sample size may have limited our ability to detect significant differences between groups. Additionally, the present study did not assess tobacco use or caffeine use disorders, which may also be relevant substances for ED groups, given their association with appetite suppression. Further, although the present sample included males and non-binary individuals, the smaller numbers in these groups limits the generalizability of the results beyond females. Importantly, we did not assess the past history of SUD, so the relative influences of active substance use versus traits underlying substance use on our findings cannot be determined. Finally, this study reviewed factors that provide a rationale for the applicability of DBT to treat EDs and co-occurring substance use in a cross-sectional study; however, future longitudinal studies and randomized controlled trials are needed to examine outcomes to determine the efficacy of DBT to treat ED-SUDs.

Conclusions

In summary, the present study found significant differences between patients with co-occurring ED-SUD and ED alone in the areas of temperament, psychiatric comorbidities, prescribed medications, and emotion regulation abilities. These significant differences may be important in guiding attempts to tailor treatment for this complex patient population and provide further evidence for the importance of integrated treatment to comprehensively address presenting problems. DBT for SUDs is a promising treatment to concurrently treat SUDs and EDs, but more research on its efficacy in the treatment of ED-SUD will be essential for establishing guidelines for treatment protocols with this patient population.

Funding

This research did not receive any specific grant from funding agencies in the public, commercial, or not-for-profit sectors. Dr. Reilly receives support from the Hilda and Preston Davis Foundation.

ORCID

Erin Reilly http://orcid.org/0000-0001-9269-0747

References

Anestis, M. D., Smith, A. R., Fink, E. L., & Joiner, T. E. (2009). Dysregulated eating and distress: Examining the specific role of negative urgency in a clinical sample. *Cognitive Therapy and Research*, *33*(4), 390–397. https://doi.org/10.1007/s10608-008-9201-2

Bahji, A., Mazhar, M. N., Hawken, E., Hudson, C. C., Nadkarni, P., & MacNeil, B. A. (2019). Prevalence of substance use disorder comorbidity among individuals with eating disorders: A systematic review and meta-analysis. *Psychiatry Research*, *273*, 58–66. https://doi.org/10.1016/j.psychres.2019.01.007

Beck, A. T., Steer, R. A., & Brown, G. K. (1996). *Beck depression inventory-II*. Psychological Corporation.

Becker, D. F., & Grilo, C. M. (2015). Comorbidity of mood and substance use disorders in patients with binge-eating disorder: Associations with personality disorder and eating disorder pathology. *Journal of Psychosomatic Research*, *79*(2), 159–164. https://doi.org/10.1016/j.jpsychores.2015.01.016

Blinder, B. J., Cumella, E. J., & Sanathara, V. A. (2006). Psychiatric comorbidities of female inpatients with eating disorders. *Psychosomatic Medicine*, *68*(3), 454–462. https://doi.org/10.1097/01.psy.0000221254.77675.f5

Compton, W. M., Thomas, Y. F., Stinson, F. S., & Grant, B. F. (2007). Prevalence, correlates, disability, and comorbidity of DSM-IV drug abuse and dependence in the United States: Results from the national epidemiologic survey on alcohol and related conditions. *Archives of General Psychiatry*, *64*(5), 566–576. https://doi.org/10.1001/archpsyc.64.5.566

Courbasson, C., Nishikawa, Y., & Dixon, L. (2012). Outcome of dialectical behaviour therapy for concurrent eating and substance use disorders. *Clinical Psychology & Psychotherapy*, *19*(5), 434–449. https://doi.org/10.1002/cpp.v19.5

Courbasson, C. M., Smith, P. D., & Cleland, P. A. (2005). Substance use disorders, anorexia, bulimia, and concurrent disorders. *Canadian Journal of Public Health*, *9*(2), 102–106. https://doi.org/10.1007/BF03403670

Dawe, S., & Loxton, N. J. (2004). The role of impulsivity in the development of substance use and eating disorders. *Neuroscience & Biobehavioral Reviews, 28*(3), 343–351. https://doi.org/10.1016/j.neubiorev.2004.03.007

Dennis, A. B., & Helfman, B. L. (2010). Managing the eating disorder patient with a comorbid substance use disorder. In M. Maine, B. H. McGilley, & D. W. Bunnell (Eds.), *Treatment of eating disorders* (pp. 233–249). Elsevier. https://doi.org/10.1016/B978-0-12-375668-8.10014-2

Dennis, A. B., Pryor, T., & Brewerton, T. D. (2014). Integrated treatment principles and strategies for patients with eating disorders, substance use disorder, and addictions. In T. D. Brewerton & A. B. Dennis (Eds.), *Eating disorders, addictions and substance use disorders* (pp. 461–489). Springer. https://doi.org/10.1007/978-3-642-45378-6_21

Dimeff, L. A., & Linehan, M. M. (2008). Dialectical behavior therapy for substance abusers. *Addiction Science & Clinical Practice, 4*(2), 39. https://doi.org/10.1151/ascp

Dir, A. L., Karyadi, K., & Cyders, M. A. (2013). The uniqueness of negative urgency as a common risk factor for self-harm behaviors, alcohol consumption, and eating problems. *Addictive Behaviors, 38*(5), 2158–2162. https://doi.org/10.1016/j.addbeh.2013.01.025

Drake, R., Essock, S., Shaner, A., Carey, K., Minkoff, K., Kola, L., Rickards, L., Lynde, D., Osher, F. C., & Clark, R. E. (2001). Implementing dual diagnosis services for clients with severe mental illness. *Psychiatric Services, 52*(4), 469–476. https://doi.org/10.1176/appi.ps.52.4.469

Fairburn, C. G., & Beglin, S. J. (1994). Assessment of eating disorders: Interview or self-report questionnaire? *International Journal of Eating Disorders, 16*(4), 363–370. https://doi.org/10.1002/1098-108X(199412)16:4<363::AID-EAT2260160405>3.0.CO;2-%23 Retrieved from https://www.ncbi.nlm.nih.gov/pubmed/7866415

First, M. B., Williams, J., & Spitzer, R. L. (2015). *Structured clinical interview for DSM-5—research version (SCID-5 for DSM-5, research version; SCID-5-RV)*. American Psychiatric Association.

Fischer, S., Settles, R., Collins, B., Gunn, R., & Smith, G. T. (2012). The role of negative urgency and expectancies in problem drinking and disordered eating: Testing a model of comorbidity in pathological and at-risk samples. *Psychology of Addictive Behaviors, 26*(1), 112–123. https://doi.org/10.1037/a0023460

Fouladi, F., Mitchell, J. E., Crosby, R. D., Engel, S. G., Crow, S., Hill, L., Le Grange, D., Powers, P., & Steffen, K. J. (2015). Prevalence of alcohol and other substance use in patients with eating disorders. *European Eating Disorders Review, 23*(6), 531–536. https://doi.org/10.1002/erv.2410

Glasner-Edwards, S., Mooney, L. J., Marinelli-Casey, P., Hillhouse, M., Ang, A., Rawson, R., & Authors, M. T. P. C. (2011). Bulimia nervosa among methamphetamine dependent adults: Association with outcomes three years after treatment. *Eating Disorders, 19*(3), 259–269. https://doi.org/10.1080/10640266.2011.566149

Gratz, K. L., & Roemer, L. (2004). Multidimensional assessment of emotion regulation and dysregulation: Development, factor structure, and initial validation of the difficulties in emotion regulation scale. *Journal of Psychopathology and Behavioral Assessment, 26*(1), 41–54. https://doi.org/10.1023/B:JOBA.0000007455.08539.94

Grilo, C. M., Becker, D. F., Walker, M. L., Levy, K. N., Edell, W. S., & McGLASHAN, T. H. (1995). Psychiatric comorbidity in adolescent inpatients with substance use disorders. *Journal of the American Academy of Child & Adolescent Psychiatry, 34*(8), 1085–1091. https://doi.org/10.1097/00004583-199508000-00019

Harned, M. S., Korslund, K. E., Foa, E. B., & Linehan, M. M. (2012). Treating PTSD in suicidal and self-injuring women with borderline personality disorder: Development and preliminary evaluation of a dialectical behavior therapy prolonged exposure protocol. *Behaviour Research and Therapy*, *50*(6), 381–386. https://doi.org/10.1016/j.brat.2012.02.011

Harris, C., & Barraclough, B. (1998). Excess mortality of mental disorder. *The British Journal of Psychiatry*, *173*(1), 11–53. https://doi.org/10.1192/bjp.173.1.11

Harrop, E. N., & Marlatt, G. A. (2010). The comorbidity of substance use disorders and eating disorders in women: Prevalence, etiology, and treatment. *Addictive Behaviors*, *35*(5), 392–398. https://doi.org/10.1016/j.addbeh.2009.12.016

Keel, P. K., Mitchell, J. E., Miller, K. B., Davis, T. L., & Crow, S. J. (1999). Long-term outcome of bulimia nervosa. *Archives of General Psychiatry*, *56*(1), 63–69. https://doi.org/10.1001/archpsyc.56.1.63

Kirkpatrick, R., Booij, L., Vance, A., Marshall, B., Kanellos-Sutton, M., Marchand, P., & Khalid-Khan, S. (2019). Eating disorders and substance use in adolescents: How substance users differ from nonsubstance users in an outpatient eating disorders treatment clinic. *International Journal of Eating Disorders*, *52*(2), 175–182. https://doi.org/10.1002/eat.v52.2

Kober, H. (2014). Emotion regulation in substance use disorders. In J. J. Gross (Ed.), *Handbook of emotion regulation* (pp. 428–446). Guilford Press.

Krug, I., Pinheiro, A. P., Bulik, C., Jiménez-Murcia, S., Granero, R., Penelo, E., … Fernández-Aranda, F. (2009). Lifetime substance abuse, family history of alcohol abuse/dependence and novelty seeking in eating disorders: Comparison study of eating disorder subgroups. *Psychiatry and Clinical Neurosciences*, *63*(1), 82–87. https://doi.org/10.1111/pcn.2009.63.issue-1

Lavender, J. M., Wonderlich, S. A., Engel, S. G., Gordon, K. H., Kaye, W. H., & Mitchell, J. E. (2015). Dimensions of emotion dysregulation in anorexia nervosa and bulimia nervosa: A conceptual review of the empirical literaure. *Clinical Psychology*, *40*, 111–122. https://doi.org/10.1016/j.cpr.2015.05.01022

Lindblad, R., Hu, L., Oden, N., Wakim, P., Rosa, C., & VanVeldhuisen, P. (2016). Mortality rates among substance use disorder participants in clinical trials: Pooled analysis of twenty-two clinical trials within the national drug abuse treatment clinical trials network. *Journal of Substance Abuse Treatment*, *70*, 73–80. https://doi.org/10.1016/j.jsat.2016.08.010

Linehan, M. (1993). *Cognitive-behavioral treatment of borderline personality disorder*. Guilford press.

Loxton, N. J., & Dawe, S. (2001). Alcohol abuse and dysfunctional eating in adolescent girls: The influence of individual differences in sensitivity to reward and punishment. *International Journal of Eating Disorders*, *29*(4), 455–462. https://doi.org/10.1002/()1098-108X

Mobbs, O., Iglesias, K., Golay, A., & Van der Linden, M. (2011). Cognitive deficits in obese persons with and without binge eating disorder: Investigation using a mental flexibility task. *Appetite*, *57*(1), 263–271. https://doi.org/10.1016/j.appet.2011.04.023

Neacsiu, A. D., Bohus, M., & Linehan, M. M. (2014). Dialectical behavior therapy: An intervention for emotion dysregulation. In J. J. Gross (Ed.), *Handbook of emotion regulation* (pp. 491–507). Guilford Press.

Pennay, A., Cameron, J., Reichert, T., Strickland, H., Lee, N. K., Hall, K., & Lubman, D. I. (2011). A systematic review of interventions for co-occurring substance use disorder and borderline personality disorder. *Journal of Substance Abuse Treatment*, *41*(4), 363–373. https://doi.org/10.1016/j.jsat.2011.05.004

Pfohl, B., Blum, N., St. John, D., McCormick, B., Allen, J., & Black, D. W. (2009). Reliability and validity of the borderline evaluation of severity over time (BEST): A self-rated scale to measure severity and change in persons with borderline personality disorder. *Journal of Personality Disorders*, *23*(3), 281–293. https://doi.org/10.1521/pedi.2009.23.3.281

Preti, A., de Girolamo, G., Vilagut, G., Alonso, J., de Graaf, R., Bruffaerts, R., Demyttenaere, K., Pinto-Meza, A., Haro, J. M., & Morosini, P. (2009). The epidemiology of eating disorders in six

European countries: Results of the ESEMeD-WMH project. *Journal of Psychiatric Research, 43* (14), 1125–1132. https://doi.org/10.1016/j.jpsychires.2009.04.003

Roerig, J. L., Mitchell, J. E., de Zwaan, M., Wonderlich, S. A., Kamran, S., Engbloom, S., Burgard, M., & Lancaster, K. (2003). The eating disorders medicine cabinet revisited: A clinician's guide to appetite suppressants and diuretics. *International Journal of Eating Disorders, 33*(4), 443–457. https://doi.org/10.1002/()1098-108X

Root, T. L., Pisetsky, E. M., Thornton, L., Lichtenstein, P., Pedersen, N. L., & Bulik, C. M. (2010). Patterns of co-morbidity of eating disorders and substance use in Swedish females. *Psychological Medicine, 40*(1), 105–115. https://doi.org/10.1017/S0033291709005662

Safer, D. L., Telch, C. F., & Agras, W. S. (2001). Dialectical behavior therapy for bulimia nervosa. *American Journal of Psychiatry, 158*(4), 632–634. https://doi.org/10.1176/appi.ajp.158.4.632

Sheehan, D. V., Lecrubier, Y., Sheehan, K. H., Amorim, P., Janavs, J., Weiller, E., Hergueta, T., Baker, R., & Dunbar, G. C. (1998). The mini-international neuropsychiatric interview (M.I.N.I.): The development and validation of a structured diagnostic psychiatric interview for DSM-IV and ICD-10. *Journal of Clinical Psychiatry, 59*(Suppl 20), 22–33. Retrieved from https://www.ncbi.nlm.nih.gov/pubmed/9881538

Spielberger, C. D., Gorsuch, R. L., & Lushene, R. (1970). *Manual for the state-trait anxiety inventory (self-evaluation questionnaire)*. Consulting Psychologists Press.

Steffen, K. J., Mitchell, J. E., Roerig, J. L., & Lancaster, K. L. (2007). The eating disorders medicine cabinet revisited: A clinician's guide to ipecac and laxatives. *International Journal of Eating Disorders, 40*(4), 360–368. https://doi.org/10.1002/()1098-108X

Telch, C. F., Agras, W. S., & Linehan, M. M. (2001). Dialectical behavior therapy for binge eating disorder. *Journal of Consulting and Clinical Psychology, 69*(6), 1061. https://doi.org/10.1037/0022-006X.69.6.1061

Torrubia, R., Avila, C., Moltó, J., & Caseras, X. (2001). The sensitivity to punishment and sensitivity to reward questionnaire (SPSRQ) as a measure of gray's anxiety and impulsivity dimensions. *Personality and Individual Differences, 31*(6), 837–862. https://doi.org/10.1016/S0191-8869(00)00183-5

Trottier, K., & MacDonald, D. E. (2017). Update on psychological trauma, other severe adverse experiences and eating disorders: State of the research and future research directions. *Current Psychiatry Reports, 19*(8), 45. https://doi.org/10.1007/s11920-017-0806-6

Self-criticism longitudinally predicts nonsuicidal self-injury in eating disorders

Natalie M. Perkins, Shelby N. Ortiz, and April R. Smith

ABSTRACT

Dialectical Behavior Therapy (DBT) has long been successfully applied to such behaviors such as nonsuicidal self-injury (NSSI) and more recently, bulimic behaviors. However, it is less clear how patients experiencing these comorbid symptoms may benefit from this treatment modality. Self-criticism, defined as a highly negative attitude towards the self, has been implicated in both EDs and NSSI and is amenable to DBT; thus, further examination of this construct may be beneficial in informing DBT treatment approaches. However, research has only examined these relationships cross-sectionally and no published research has examined self-criticism as a longitudinal predictor of NSSI and ED symptoms. Thus, this study examined self-criticism as a potential driving factor of NSSI in EDs in order to inform treatments, particularly DBT. Data were collected from 92 treatment-seeking adults at ED treatment facilities in the United States. Participants self-reported ED pathology, NSSI engagement, and self-criticism at baseline and a two-month follow-up. A path analysis revealed that self-criticism at baseline was associated with NSSI frequency at follow-up over and above baseline NSSI and ED symptomology. Self-criticism at baseline was not associated with ED pathology at follow-up. Self-criticism longitudinally predicted NSSI, but not ED pathology, in an ED sample. As such, it may be important for clinicians to assess for self-criticism and consider treatments that target both self-criticism and self-injury, like DBT, for this population.

Clinical Implications

- Adults with an eating disorder who are highly self-critical were at risk for future self-injury
- Using DBT with clients who are highly self-critical may be useful for managing and preventing future self-injury
- Results support using a DBT framework when working with individuals who engage in disordered eating and self-injury behaviors

Nonsuicidal self-injury (NSSI) is common among those with eating disorders (EDs; Claes et al., 2015; Claes & Muehlenkamp, 2014; Svirko &

Hawton, 2007), with studies finding NSSI is almost twice as common in those with EDs compared to other psychiatric disorders (Favaro & Santonastaso, 2000). Further, studies have estimated that between 5-35% of individuals with EDs have engaged in NSSI (Gratz, 2001; Nada-Raja, Skegg, Langley, Morrison, & Sowerby, 2004; Whitlock et al., 2011). Theoretical work from Muehlenkamp, Peat, Claes, and Smits (2012) suggests that both NSSI and EDs are disorders of emotion regulation, perhaps explaining why these behaviors so often occur in tandem. Dialectical behavior therapy (DBT) was originally developed to treat NSSI and suicidal behavior in individuals with borderline personality disorder (BPD) but has since been used more broadly to address pervasive patterns of emotion dysregulation and associated maladaptive behaviors (Linehan, 1993). DBT has also been successfully modified to treat EDs (Lynch et al., 2013; Safer, Telch, & Agras, 2001; Telch, Agras, & Linehan, 2001) and has been found to be effective in treating bulimic and suicidal behaviors and NSSI (Fischer & Peterson, 2015). However, in order to continue to adapt this approach to the treatment of comorbid NSSI and EDs, we need to better understand mechanisms driving NSSI within this population. Self-criticism has been implicated in both EDs and NSSI; thus the current study examined self-criticism as a driving factor of NSSI in EDs to inform treatments geared toward treating self-harm, like DBT.

Self-criticism has been defined as a highly negative attitude towards the self (St. Germain & Hooley, 2012). Self-criticism is often considered a maladaptive emotion regulation strategy (Gross, 1998), wherein individuals with heightened levels of psychopathology report greater usage of self-criticism in response to negative emotion across multiple contexts (Aldao & Nolen-Hoeksema, 2012). Specifically, self-criticism, in combination with the experience of stronger negative emotions and an inability to use more adaptive emotion regulation strategies, has been associated with more frequent and severe depressive episodes (Gilbert, Clarke, Hempel, Miles, & Irons, 2004). Self-criticism is also associated with greater contempt and disgust for the self and is linked to more severe ED pathology (Fennig et al., 2008; Gilbert et al., 2004; Kelly & Carter, 2013) and body dissatisfaction, wherein ED patients are more likely to be dissatisfied with their bodies and overvaluate shape and weight if they are more self-critical (Dunkley & Grilo, 2006; Dunkley, Masheb, & Grilo, 2010). Similar work in EDs has also examined self-critical perfectionism, defined as a maladaptive version of perfectionism (Frost, Marten, Lahart, & Rosenblate, 1990; Hamachek, 1978). This tendency towards maladaptive or self-critical perfectionism has been repeatedly found to increase risk for EDs (Bardone-Cone et al., 2007; Wade, Wilksch, Paxton, Byrne, & Austin, 2015). Furthermore, maladaptive perfectionism, which has been repeatedly implicated in the development and maintenance of EDs, was found to be partially explained by high levels of self-criticism (Dunkley, Blankstein, Masheb, & Grilo, 2006). Recent longitudinal work found that self-critical perfectionism prospectively predicted binge eating symptoms in adolescents (Boone, Vansteenkiste, Soenens, Van der Kaapdeeder, & Verstuyf, 2014). However, it remains less clear how self-criticism may influence the development of comorbidities like NSSI in EDs.

Individuals that self-injure have been repeatedly shown to be more self-critical than individuals that do not engage in NSSI (Glassman, Weierich, Hooley, Deliberto, & Nock, 2007; St. Germain & Hooley, 2012). Self-criticism is also robustly associated with more frequent and severe self-injury (Gilbert et al., 2010; Xavier, Gouveia, & Cunha, 2016). St. Germain and Hooley (2012) theorized that self-criticism facilitates self-injury by removing a barrier to more extreme and maladaptive forms of self-punishment (Hooley & Franklin, 2018; Nock, 2009; St. Germain & Hooley, 2012). Specifically, holding a low regard for the self may allow a person to consider and later use more maladaptive versions of emotion regulation, including self-injury. This mechanism may also apply to disordered eating, which has been conceptualized as an indirect form of self-injury (St. Germain & Hooley, 2012).

Few longitudinal studies have examined the temporal relationship between self-criticism and NSSI. However, exploratory studies have noted that self-criticism appears to predict future NSSI engagement above and beyond more well-established predictors, such as depression and anxiety (Xavier et al., 2016). In other longitudinal work, You, Lin, and Leung (2015) found that the moderating effect of negative emotions between BPD symptoms and future NSSI engagement was stronger when self-criticism was high. Similarly, self-hatred, an extreme form of self-criticism, significantly increased the odds of engaging in NSSI in a sample of adolescents and young adults in a study using ecological momentary assessments (Nock, Prinstein, & Sterba, 2010). Experimental work has also shown that decreasing self-criticism lessened subsequent pain tolerance in adults reporting current NSSI (Hooley & St. Germain, 2014). Overall, this research indicates that greater self-criticism may increase risk for NSSI. However, further longitudinal work is needed, particularly in ED populations, to understand whether self-criticism may relate to both NSSI and EDs symptoms.

Based on the existing literature, it appears likely that high levels of self-criticism observed in individuals with EDs may put them at risk for NSSI engagement. Claes and Muehlenkamp (2014) proposed a model in which self-criticism is a specific risk factor for both NSSI and EDs. Claes, Soenens, Vanstennkiste, and Vandereycken (2012) have also shown that perfectionism, along with parental criticism, is associated with NSSI engagement in EDs. However, to the authors' knowledge, no research to date has examined whether self-criticism is a longitudinal risk factor for NSSI within an ED population.

Rationale

Self-criticism appears to play a key role in the development and maintenance of both NSSI and EDs. Given the centrality of this construct to both behaviors, it may explain their high rates of comorbidity and be a useful factor in identifying individuals with EDs who are at risk for future NSSI engagement and in need of specialized treatments that target these behaviors, like DBT. Based on previous research, we hypothesized that among individual with EDs, self-criticism would longitudinally predict NSSI engagement and symptoms of disordered eating above and beyond previous NSSI engagement and disordered eating.

Method

The present study is a secondary analysis of data collected for the longitudinal study detailed in Smith, Forrest, Velkoff, Ribeiro, and Franklin (2018). All study procedures received approval from the University's Institutional Review Board.

Participants

Participants in this study were 92 adults with EDs who were recruited from treatment facilities throughout the U.S. Using diagnostic criteria from the 5th edition of the *Diagnostic and Statistical Manual of Mental Disorders* (*DSM*; American Psychiatric Association, 2013), approximately one-third of the sample (n = 32) had AN/subthreshold AN, 40% of the sample (n = 37) had BN/subthreshold BN, and the rest of the sample had BED/subthreshold BED (n = 12), purging disorder (n= 3), night eating syndrome (n= 7), and unspecified feeding/eating disorder (n= 1). The sample primarily identified as White (93.5%) and female (96%), and ranged in age from 18–62 (M = 32.35; SD = 11.35).

Procedure

Flyers posted at ED treatment facilities were used to inform patients of the study. Patients interested in participating completed a pre-screening online survey that assessed ED symptomatology. Only patients with active symptoms were invited by e-mail to participate. Following the prescreening questionnaire, 110 individuals were eligible to complete the study. Ninety-two individuals provided consent and completed the baseline assessment. Seventy-five of those individuals completed the follow-up assessment (81.5%). A secure online survey platform was used to collect data at baseline and then two months following baseline. Participants were compensated with Amazon gift cards for survey completion.

Measures

ED diagnosis

The Eating Disorder Diagnostic Scale-DSM-5 Version (EDDS-5; Stice, n.d., http://ww.orr.org/sticemeasures) is a self-report measure made up of 23 items that assess *DSM-5* ED diagnostic criteria over the past three months. This measure has high internal consistency and convergent validity with the Eating Disorder Examination (EDE; Cooper & Fairburn, 1987) and was administered at baseline to assign diagnosis. To further verify diagnoses, symptoms endorsed on the EDDS-5 were corroborated against other self-reported ED symptoms and body mass index (BMI), see Smith et al. (2018) for additional details.

ED symptoms

ED symptoms were also measured at baseline and follow-up using the Eating Disorder Inventory (EDI; Garner, Olmstead, & Polivy, 1983). This questionnaire contained 64 items and was measured using a 6-point scale ranging from 1 *(Never)* to 6 *(Always)*. Although the original scoring algorithm has each item be weighted from 0 to 3, the method we used in the present study (1 to 6) is often used in research to increase variance in participant scores. The three primary factors of the EDI that relate to disordered eating are: drive for thinness (e.g., *I am terrified of gaining weight*; baseline alpha = .82; follow-up alpha = .84), bulimia (e.g., *I eat or drink in secrecy*; baseline alpha = .89; follow-up alpha = .87), and body dissatisfaction (e.g., *I think that my thighs are too large*; baseline alpha = .89; follow-up alpha = .85). Mean scores for each subscale were similar to previously published data from a clinical ED sample with a history of NSSI (Claes et al., 2018).

Self-injurious behaviors

The Functional Assessment of Self-Mutilation (Lloyd, Kelly, & Hope, 1997) was used to obtain self-reported information on the frequency and functions of self-injurious behavior. The measure includes eleven items assessing the number of times various types of self-injurious behavior (e.g., "cutting/burning/scraping skin") were performed during the past year and if medical treatment was required. Frequency of each type of NSSI was summed to create a score for the total number of times participants engaged in NSSI. When the measure was administered at follow-up, questions were altered to assess engagement in self-injurious behavior over the past month. Mean past month NSSI frequency was significantly elevated compared to previously published data in adult samples (Anestis et al., 2012; Muehlenkamp et al.,

2012; Turner, Yiu, Claes, Muehlenkamp, & Chapman, 2016). However, given the clinical nature of the current sample, this elevation was expected.

Self-criticism

The Self-Rating Scale (SRS; Hooley, Ho, Slater, & Lockshin, 2010) was used to assess self-criticism by having individuals rate statements such as "*sometimes I feel completely worthless*" and "*others are justified in criticizing me.*" The eight-item scale uses a 7-point Likert scale ranging from *Strongly Disagree* to *Strongly Agree.* This measure has demonstrated good internal reliability in previous studies (e.g., Glassman et al., 2007) and excellent internal reliability in the current study (baseline alpha = .92; follow-up alpha = .90). Mean self-criticism scores were similar to, if not slightly elevated compared to previously published data from a self-injuring sample with elevated disordered eating (St. Germain & Hooley, 2012). However, given that the current study utilized a clinical sample, this elevation in SRS scores was expected. It should be noted that in the current study, scores on the SRS were obtained by taking the mean of all items, whereas for previous samples, SRS scores were calculated by simply summing responses to each item (St. Germain & Hooley, 2012).

Data analytic strategy

A path analysis was conducted in Mplus version 7.3 (Muthén & Muthén,). The NSSI frequency variables demonstrated significant kurtosis, which is normal for these types of variables. Given this, the baseline and follow-up NSSI frequency variables were windsorised based on the 95th percentile (161 acts at baseline, 48 acts at follow-up; Ammerman, Jacobucci, & McCloskey, 2018). The resulting distributions were still somewhat non-normal (skewness [2.03–3.06], kurtosis [3.09–8.45], thus robust estimators (i.e., MLR) were used. Missing data were relatively minimal as the covariance coverage matrix indicated that the proportion of pairwise present data ranged from .72-.97. Missing data were handled using full information maximum likelihood (FIML) which is considered to be the best technique for handling missing data (Enders, 2010). SPSS was used for descriptives, computing correlations, and computing reliabilities.

To conduct the path analysis, the outcome variables (past month NSSI frequency assessed at follow-up, EDI bulimia at follow-up, EDI drive for thinness at follow-up, and EDI body dissatisfaction at follow-up) were regressed on the main predictor, self-criticism, and all baseline measurements were controlled for (past year NSSI assessed at baseline, EDI bulimia at baseline, EDI drive for thinness at baseline, and EDI body dissatisfaction at baseline). Age was also controlled for as it was related to several of the variables.

Table 1. Correlations and descriptive statistics for self-criticism, eating disorder symptoms, and self-harm frequency.

N = 92	1	2	3	4	5	6	7	8	9	10
1. BL Self-Criticism	–									
2. BL EDI-Drive for Thinness	.39**	–								
3. BL EDI-Body Dissatisfaction	.38**	.57**	–							
4. BL EDI Bulimia	−.01	.01	.17	–						
5. BL Self-Harm Frequency	.14	−.11	.05	.11	–					
6. FU Self-Criticism	.80**	.31*	.25*	−.14	.15	–				
7. FU EDI-Drive for Thinness	.26*	.74**	.39**	.02	−.15	.38*	–			
8. FU EDI-Body Dissatisfaction	.44**	.44**	.82*	.23	−.05	.37**	.48**	–		
9. FU EDI Bulimia	−.05	−.01	.27**	.84**	.02	−.02	.17	.31**	–	
10. FU Self-Harm Frequency	.33**	−.08	.16	.26*	.24	.33**	.05	.16	.23	–
Mean	4.67	33.88	44.87	22.00	32.65	4.39	31.79	43.60	20.71	5.56
Standard deviation	1.33	6.01	8.57	8.65	76.13	1.46	6.82	7.68	7.52	15.03

Note. * $p < .05$ ** $p < .01$; *** $p < .001$. BL = baseline. EDI = Eating Disorder Inventory. FU = follow-up.

Results

Descriptive statistics and correlations are reported from the original data (see Table 1). Baseline self-criticism scores were positively and significantly correlated with EDI drive for thinness (baseline and follow-up), EDI body dissatisfaction (baseline and follow-up) and self-harm frequency at follow-up. All correlations were small to moderate in magnitude (*r*'s = .26- .44).

The path model revealed that our hypotheses were only partially confirmed. Specifically, baseline self-criticism was significantly associated with NSSI frequency at follow-up (β = .29, SE = .09, *p* = .002), over and above baseline NSSI frequency and all ED variables. However, controlling for the other variables, self-criticism was not a significant longitudinal predictor of any of the ED variables (*p*'s = .21-.94). As might be expected, all the ED subscales predicted one another, but they only predicted their respective subscale (e.g., baseline drive for thinness predicted drive for thinness at follow-up). None of the ED subscales predicted NSSI at follow-up (*p*'s = .13-.80). See Figure 1 for the path model results.

Discussion

Previous research has established the relationship between self-criticism and NSSI; however, the current study is the first to examine self-criticism as

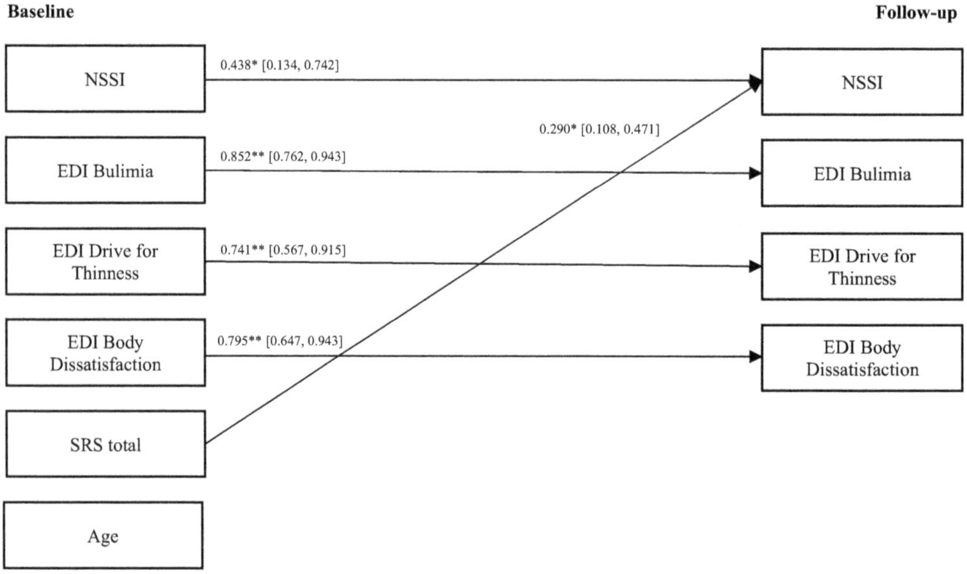

Figure 1. Path analysis model showing the relationship between self-criticism, NSSI, and eating disorder symptoms. Significant paths are indicated by solid lines. Path values represent standardized path regression weights with 95% confidence intervals in square brackets. *p < .01, **p < .001. NSSI = nonsuicidal self-injury; EDI = Eating Disorder Inventory, multiple subscales; SRS = Self Rating Scale.

a longitudinal predictor of NSSI in an ED sample. Partially supporting study hypotheses, self-criticism at baseline uniquely predicted NSSI frequency at follow-up. However, contrary to study hypotheses, self-criticism at baseline did not predict ED pathology at follow-up, despite cross-sectional associations with ED pathology at baseline and follow-up.

This study is the first study to the authors' knowledge to provide evidence supporting self-criticism as a longitudinal predictor of NSSI frequency above and beyond known predictors of NSSI frequency, like previous NSSI engagement and disordered eating, in an ED sample. Previous NSSI engagement has been repeatedly found to be one of the strongest predictors of future NSSI engagement (Fox et al., 2015). Thus, these results highlight the importance of self-criticism to NSSI engagement among ED patients, as self-criticism remained a robust predictor of NSSI engagement over and above previous NSSI engagement. Past research has found that highly self-critical adults more frequently engage in NSSI (Xavier et al., 2016). However, this study is the first to replicate this finding in an ED sample. Self-criticism is often linked to self-punishment, wherein individuals who are highly self-critical use NSSI as a method of self-punishment (Hooley & Franklin, 2018; Nock, 2009; St. Germain & Hooley, 2012). Given that individuals with EDs are highly self-critical to begin with (Fennig et al., 2008; Kelly & Carter, 2013), this may put them at an increased risk for NSSI.

Contrary to our hypotheses, self-criticism was not related to ED pathology longitudinally after controlling for other variables; however, it was related to ED pathology cross-sectionally. These discrepant findings may be due to a number of factors. First, self-criticism is known to influence core ED cognitions, including body dissatisfaction (Dunkley & Grilo, 2006; Dunkley et al., 2010). These core ED cognitions captured in the current study's assessments may account for the greatest proportion of ED pathology risk. Although self-criticism may play a role in these cognitions, it is likely one of many other important factors, and thus, perhaps not a central risk factor for ED pathology. Second, though ED pathology has been repeatedly associated with maladaptive or self-critical perfectionism, less work has specifically examined self-criticism in EDs longitudinally. Thus, our discrepant findings could in part be due to the assessment of self-criticism as opposed to self-critical or maladaptive perfectionism. Third, there was little variance in ED symptoms across the two time points. Therefore, it is possible that after controlling for baseline ED symptoms, there was not enough additional variance that could have been predicted by self-criticism. The current study's length of assessment may not have allowed for enough variance in ED symptoms to emerge; thus, it is possible that a longer assessment period may have yielded differing results.

Practice considerations

The longitudinal nature of these findings suggests that adults with an ED who are highly self-critical may be at risk for future NSSI engagement. As previously discussed, self-hatred is thought to remove a potential barrier to the usage of NSSI as a more extreme form of self-punishment (Hooley & Franklin, 2018; Nock, 2009; St. Germain & Hooley, 2012). Therefore, it may be useful for clinicians to periodically assess self-criticism to monitor and address this risk as needed. As previously discussed, self-criticism is often considered a maladaptive emotion regulation strategy. Given DBT's strong focus on improving emotion regulation by reducing the usage of such maladaptive strategies (Linehan, 1993), we believe this highly critical population would especially benefit from this intervention. In addition, using this approach with clients who are highly self-critical may be useful for managing this risk as well as for preventing future NSSI engagement. A recent study examining the effectiveness of DBT for adolescents endorsing current binging and purging, as well as NSSI and suicidal behavior, found that at a 6-month follow-up, the majority of patients were not currently engaging in NSSI and nearly half were not currently binge-eating (Fischer & Peterson, 2015). Overall, the results from this study can be interpreted as support for using a DBT framework when working with individuals who engage in disordered eating and NSSI behaviors. Specifically, many emotion regulation skills, such as acting opposite when urges to self-injure occur, and mindfulness skills, such as fostering compassionate thoughts towards the self, may prove especially beneficial for highly self-critical individuals (Linehan, 2015).

Additionally, radically open DBT (RO-DBT; Lynch et al., 2013; Safer et al., 2001; Telch et al., 2001), which was developed to address emotionally over-controlled tendencies (i.e., overly inhibited, perfectionistic, and cautious), may be effective for individuals with more restrictive ED symptoms resembling anorexia nervosa. Over-control has been repeatedly linked to maladaptive perfectionism, a form of self-criticism (Anderluh, Tchanturia, Rabe-Hesketh, Collier, & Treasure, 2009). Thus, by targeting over-control, reductions in self-criticism and NSSI risk may also be seen in this subset of individuals displaying ED symptoms. Furthermore, as DBT was originally developed in part to address NSSI engagement, modifications of this treatment such as RO-DBT may be particularly useful in treating restrictive disordered eating and NSSI comorbidity.

Limitations

Although these results expand the field's understanding or the importance of self-critici, the current study is not without limitations. First, the study used a relatively small sample size ($n= 92$). Despite the strength of this study's main findings, these results would benefit from replication with a larger sample size. Second, participants were treatment-seeking adults recruited from ED treatment facilities. Although the use of a clinical sample greatly increases the base rate of the behaviors under investigation, the use of a clinical sample limits the generalizability of the results because treatment-seeking adults may differ from non-treatment-seeking adults on the variables of interest (e.g., Forrest, Smith, & Swanson, 2017). Lastly, all data were collected via self-report measures. An additional limitation was that we did not have information on what phase of treatment or level of care these individuals were at when completing the study.

Conclusions

Despite these limitations, the current study has several strengths. The study utilized path analysis, which allows for the examination of multiple relations between variables at the same time. This study is also one of very few longitudinal studies examining predictors of NSSI in ED samples. Given that engagement in NSSI greatly increases risk of physical injury and fatal self-injury (Andover & Gibb, 2010; Ribeiro et al., 2016) in a group with already impaired physical health, it is crucial to further understand what factors may beget NSSI. Moreover, the assessment of past month NSSI frequency allows for greater prediction accuracy. Overall, the current study provides evidence that self-criticism may be a unique risk factor for NSSI in ED samples beyond other known risk factors. Clinically, these results suggest that targeting self-critical thinking in therapy may reduce risk for future NSSI engagement in clients with ED pathology. In particular, these results suggest that adults engaging in both disordered eating and NSSI may be a good fit for and especially responsive to DBT, given that this approach can address both behaviors simultaneously.

ORCID

Natalie M. Perkins http://orcid.org/0000-0003-2773-0778
Shelby N. Ortiz http://orcid.org/0000-0001-8088-8254

References

Aldao, A., & Nolen-Hoeksema, S. (2012). The influence of context on the implementation of adaptive emotion regulation strategies. *Behaviour Research and Therapy*, *50*, 493–501. doi:10.1016/j.brat.2012.04.004

Ammerman, B. A., Jacobucci, R., & McCloskey, M. S. (2018). Using exploratory data mining to identify important correlates of nonsuicidal self-injury frequency. *Psychology of Violence*, *8*, 515–525. doi:10.1037/vio0000146

Anderluh, M., Tchanturia, K., Rabe-Hesketh, S., Collier, D., & Treasure, J. (2009). Lifetime course of eating disorders: Design and validity testing of a new strategy to define the eating disorders phenotype. *Psychological Medicine, 39,* 105–114.

Andover, M. S., & Gibb, B. E. (2010). Non-suicidal self-injury, attempted suicide, and suicidal intent among psychiatric inpatients. *Psychiatry Research, 178,* 101–105. doi:10.1016/j.psychres.2010.03.019

Bardone-Cone, A. M., Wonderlich, S. A., Frost, R. O., Bulik, C. M., Mitchell, J. E., Uppala, S., & Simonich, H. (2007). Perfectionism and eating disorders: Current status and future directions. *Clinical Psychology Review, 27,* 384–405. doi:10.1016/j.cpr.2006.12.005

Boone, L., Vansteenkiste, M., Soenens, B., Van der Kaapdeeder, J., & Verstuyf, J. (2014). Self-critical perfectionism and binge eating symptoms: A longitudinal test of the intervening role of psychological need frustration. *Journal of Counseling Psychology, 61,* 363–373. doi:10.1037/a0036418

Claes, L., Islam, M. A., Fagundo, A. B., Jimenez-Murcia, S., Granero, R., Agüera, Z., & Fernández-Aranda, F. (2015). The relationship between non-suicidal self-injury and UPPS-P impulsivity facets in eating disorders and healthy controls. *PloS One, 1,* 1–11.

Claes, L., & Muehlenkamp, J L. Claes & J. Muehlenkamp (Eds (2014). Non-suicidal self-injury and eating disorders: dimensions of self-harm. In L. Claes & J. Muehlenkamp (Eds (Eds), *Non-suicidal self-injury in eating disorders: advancements in etiology and treatment. pp. 3-18.* Germany: Springer: Heidelberg.

Claes, L., Soenens, B., Vanstennkiste, M., & Vandereycken, W. (2012). The scars of the inner critic: Perfectionism and nonsuicidal self-injury in eating disorders. *European Eating Disorders Review, 20,* 196–202. doi:10.1002/erv.1158

Claes, L., Turner, B., Dierckx, E., Luyckx, K., Verschueren, M., & Schoevaerts, K. (2018). Different clinical presentations in eating disorder patients with non-suicidal self-injury based on the co-occurrence of borderline personality disorder. *Psychologica Belgica, 58,* 243–255. doi:10.5334/pb.420

Cooper, Z., & Fairburn, C. (1987). The eating disorder examination: A semi-structured interview for the assessement of the specific psychopathology of eating disorders. *International Journal of Eating Disorders, 6,* 1–8. doi:10.1002/1098-108X(198701)6:1<1::AID-EAT2260060102>3.0.CO;2-9

Dunkley, D. M., Blankstein, K. R., Masheb, R. M., & Grilo, C. M. (2006). Personal standards and evaluative concerns dimensions of "clinical" perfectionism: A reply to Shafran et al. (2002, 2003) and Hewitt et al. (2003). *Behaviour Research and Therapy, 44,* 63–84. doi:10.1016/j.brat.2004.12.004

Dunkley, D. M., & Grilo, C. M. (2006). Self-criticism, low self-esteem, depressive symptoms, and over-evaluation of shape and weight in binge eating disorder patients. *Behaviour Research and Therapy, 45,* 139–149. doi:10.1016/j.brat.2006.01.017

Dunkley, D. M., Masheb, R. M., & Grilo, C. M. (2010). Childhood maltreatment, depressive symptoms, and body dissatisfaction in patients with binge-eating disorder: The mediating role of self-criticism. *International Journal of Eating Disorders, 43,* 274–281. doi:10.1002/eat.20796

Enders, C. K. (2010). *Applied missing data analysis.* New York, NY: Guilford press.

Favaro, A., & Santonastaso, P. (2000). Self-injurious behavior in anorexia nervosa. *The Journal of Nervous and Mental Disease, 188,* 537–542. doi:10.1097/00005053-200008000-00010

Fennig, S., Hadas, A., Itzhaky, L., Roe, D., Apter, A., & Shahar, G. (2008). Self-criticism is a key predictor of eating disorder dimensions among inpatient adolescent females. *International Journal of Eating Disorders, 41,* 762–765. doi:10.1002/eat.v41:8

Fischer, S., & Peterson, C. (2015). Dialectical behavior therapy for adolescent binge eating, purging, suicidal behavior, and non-suicidal self-injury: A pilot study. *Psychotherapy, 52*, 78–92. doi:10.1037/a0036065

Fox, K. R., Franklin, J. C., Ribeiro, J. D., Kleiman, E. M., Bentley, K. H., & Nock, M. K. (2015). Meta-analysis of risk factors for nonsuicidal self-injury. *Clinical Psychology Review, 42*, 156–167. doi:10.1016/j.cpr.2015.09.002

Frost, R. O., Marten, P., Lahart, C., & Rosenblate, R. (1990). The dimensions of perfectionism. *Cognitive Therapy and Research, 14*, 449–468. doi:10.1007/BF01172967

Garner, D. M., Olmstead, M. P., & Polivy, J. (1983). Development and validation of a multidimensional eating disorder inventory for anorexia nervosa and bulimia. *International Journal of Eating Disorders, 2*, 15–34. doi:10.1002/(ISSN)1098-108X

Gilbert, P., Clarke, M., Hempel, S., Miles, J. N. V., & Irons, C. (2004). Criticizing and reassuring oneself: An exploration of forms, styles and reasons in female students. *The British Journal of Clinical Psychology, 41*, 31–50. doi:10.1348/014466504772812959

Gilbert, P., McEwan, K., Irons, C., Bhundia, R., Christie, R., Broomhead, C., & Rockliff, H. (2010). Self-harm in a mixed clinical population: The roles of self-criticism, shame, and social rank. *British Journal of Clinical Psychology, 49*, 563–576. doi:10.1348/014466509X479771

Glassman, L. H., Weierich, M. R., Hooley, J. M., Deliberto, T. L., & Nock, M. K. (2007). Child maltreatment, non-suicidal self-injury, and the mediating role of self-criticism. *Behaviour Research and Therapy, 45*, 2483–2490. doi:10.1016/j.brat.2007.04.002

Gratz, K. L. (2001). Measurement of deliberate self-harm: Preliminary data on the eliberate Self-Harm Inventory. *Journal of Psychopathology and Behavioral Assessment, 23*, 253–263. doi:10.1023/A:1012779403943

Gross, J. J. (1998). The emerging field of emotion regulation: An integrative review. *Review of General Psychology, 2*, 271–299. doi:10.1037/1089-2680.2.3.271

Hamachek, D. E. (1978). Psychodynamics of normal and neurotic perfectionism. *Psychology, 15*, 27–33.

Hooley, J. M., & Franklin, J. C. (2018). Why do people hurt themselves? A new conceptual model of nonsuicidal self-injury. *Clinical Psychological Science, 6*, 428–451.

Hooley, J. M., Ho, D. T., Slater, J., & Lockshin, A. (2010). Pain perception and nonsuicidal self-injury: a laboratory investigation.. *Personality Disorders: Theory, Research, and Treatment, 1*, 170–179. doi:10.1037/a0020106

Hooley, J. M., & St. Germain, S. A. (2014). Nonsuicidal self-injury, pain, and self-criticism; Does changing self-worth change pain endurance in people who engage in self-injury?. *Clinical Psychological Science, 2*, 297–305. doi:10.1177/2167702613509372

Kelly, A. C., & Carter, J. C. (2013). Why self-critical patients present with more severe eating disorder pathology: The mediating role of shame. *British Journal of Clinical Psychology, 52*, 148–161. doi:10.1111/bjc.2013.52.issue-2

Linehan, M. M. (1993). *Cognitive behavioral treatment of borderline personality disorder.* New York, NY: Guilford Press.

Linehan, M. M. (2015). *DBT skills training manual* (2nd ed.). New York, NY: Guilford Press.

Lloyd, E. E., Kelly, M. L., & Hope, T. (1997). Self-mutilation in a community sample of adolescents: Descriptive characteristics and provisional prevalence rates. Poster session presented at the annual meeting of the society for Behavioral Medicine. New Orleans, LA.

Lynch, T. R., Gray, K. L. H., Hempel, R. J., Titley, M., Chen, E. Y., & O'Mahen, H. A. (2013). Radically open-dialectical behavior therapy for adult anorexia nervosa: Feasibility and outcomes from an inpatient program. *BMC Psychiatry, 13*, 1–30. doi:10.1186/1471-244X-13-1

Muehlenkamp, J. J., Peat, C. M., Claes, L., & Smits, D. (2012). Self-injury and disordered eating: Expressing emotion dysregulation through the body. *Suicide and Life-Threatening Behavior, 42,* 416–425. doi:10.1111/sltb.2012.42.issue-4

Muthén, L. K., & Muthén, B. O. (1998–2012). Mplus User's Guide. (7th ed.). Los Angeles,: Muthén & Muthén

Nada-Raja, S., Skegg, K., Langley, J., Morrison, D., & Sowerby, P. (2004). Self-harmful behaviors in a population-based sample of young adults. *Suicide and Life-Threatening Behavior, 34,* 177–186. doi:10.1521/suli.34.2.177.32781

Nock, M. K. (2009). Why do people hurt themselves? New insights in the nature and functions of self-injury. *Current Directions in Psychological Science, 18,* 78–83. doi:10.1111/j.1467-8721.2009.01613.x

Nock, M. K., Prinstein, M. J., & Sterba, S. K. (2010). Revealing the form and function of self-injurious thoughts and behaviors: A real-time ecological assessment study among adolescent and young adults. *Psychology of Violence, 1,* 36–52. doi:10.1037/2152-0828.1.S.36

Ribeiro, J. D., Franklin, J. C., Fox, K. R., Bentley, K. H., Kleimman, E. M., Chang, B. P., & Nock, M. K. (2016). Self-injurious thoughts and behaviors as risk factors for future suicide ideation, attempts, and death: A meta-analysis of longitudinal studies. *Psychological Medicine, 46,* 225–236. doi:10.1017/S0033291715001804

Safer, D. L., Telch, C. F., & Agras, W. S. (2001). Dialectical behavior therapy for bulimia nervosa. *The American Journal of Psychiatry, 158,* 632–634. doi:10.1176/appi.ajp.158.4.632

Smith, A. R., Forrest, L. N., Velkoff, E. A., Ribeiro, J. D., & Franklin, J. C. (2018). Implicit attitudes toward eating stimuli differentiate eating disorder and non-eating disorder groups and predict eating disorder behaviors. *International Journal of Eating Disorders, 51,* 343–351. doi:10.1002/eat.v51.4

St. Germain, S. A., & Hooley, J. M. (2012). Direct and indirect forms of non-suicidal self-injury: Evidence for a distinction. *Psychiatry Research, 197,* 78–84. doi:10.1016/j.psychres.2011.12.050

Svirko, E., & Hawton, K. (2007). Self-injurious behavior and eating disorders: The extent and nature of the association. *Suicide & Life-threatening Behavior, 37,* 409–421. doi:10.1521/suli.2007.37.issue-4

Telch, C. F., Agras, W. S., & Linehan, M. M. (2001). Dialectical behavior therapy for binge eating disorder. *Journal of Consulting and Clinical Psychology, 69,* 1061–1065. doi:10.1037/0022-006X.69.6.1061

Wade, T. D., Wilksch, S. M., Paxton, S. J., Byrne, S. M., & Austin, S. B. (2015). How perfectionism and ineffectiveness influence growth of eating disorder risk in young adolescent girls. *Behaviour Research and Therapy, 66,* 56–63. doi:10.1016/j.brat.2015.01.007

Whitlock, J., Muehlenkamp, J., Purington, A., Eckenrode, J., Barreira, P., Baral Abrams, G., & Knox, K. (2011). Nonsuicidal self-injury in a college population: General trens and sex differences. *Journal of American College Health, 59,* 691–698. doi:10.1080/07448481.2010.529626

Xavier, A., Gouveia, J. P., & Cunha, M. (2016). Non-suicidal self-injury in adolescence: The role of shame, self-criticism and fear of self-compassion. *Child & Youth Care Forum, 45,* 571–586. doi:10.1007/s10566-016-9346-1

You, J., Lin, M., & Leung, F. (2015). A longitudinal moderated mediation model of non-suicidal self-injury among adolescents. *Journal of Abnormal Child Psychology, 43,* 381–390. doi:10.1007/s10802-014-9901-x

Outpatient treatment for adults with complex eating disorders and co-morbid conditions: a decision making model and case example

Joanna Marino, Rebecca Hardin, Alexandra Gasbarro, Victoria A. Dansereau, and Sarah Fischer

ABSTRACT

Although Cognitive Behavioral Therapy (CBT-E) for eating disorders has the most empirical support for the outpatient treatment of adult eating disorders (EDs), this model does not include a focus on intense emotion dysregulation, suicidality, and non-suicidal self-injury (NSSI). Furthermore, a subset of patients do not achieve sustained remission with CBT-E. Given that Dialectical Behavior Therapy (DBT) was designed for treatment refractory, complex patients, clinicians must be able to use assessment information to determine which type of treatment to use. The aims of this manuscript are to 1) describe a DBT-based and research-informed conceptual model for treatment decision making for an outpatient non-academic setting, 2) present a case example of a client with significant ED symptoms and complex medical and psychiatric comorbidities, using this decision making model and 3) present descriptive data from a private practice setting in which patients are referred to DBT vs. CBT-E according to this decision making model.

Clinical implications

- When clients with eating disorders also have suicidal behavior and non-suicidal self-injury, it may be difficult for clinicians to determine what to prioritize in treatment and in each session.
- The clinical decision making model presented in this paper may aid clinicians in determining which treatment modality to use (CBT-E or DBT) with eating disorder clients who also have suicidality.
- Functional analysis of suicidal ideation, non-suicidal self-injury, past suicide attempts, and eating disorder symptoms may be more useful in selecting which treatment to use than a diagnosis.

Eating disorders (EDs) are challenging illnesses to treat. The aim of the current paper is to describe a decision making model for clients who may be referred to comprehensive DBT (DBT) as opposed to cognitive behavioral therapy for eating disorders (CBT-E) when they present for outpatient eating disorder treatment, and present data from an outpatient clinic using this model. In this paper, the rationale for this decision making model is described. A case example is also used to illustrate the difficulty in decision making regarding appropriate treatment referrals when clients with complex co-occurring symptoms present for eating disorder treatment.

Challenges in efficacious eating disorder treatment

Randomized controlled trials of CBT-E compared to other active treatments indicate that although CBT-E is efficacious, there is a large group of ED sufferers whose symptoms do not remit in treatment (Poulsen et al., 2014; Wonderlich et al., 2014). This may be due to the high rates of other psychopathology, suicidality, and non-suicidal self-injury (NSSI) that frequently co-occur with EDs (Islam et al., 2015; Kostro, Lerman, & Attia, 2014). Individuals with eating disorders commonly have difficulties across a broad spectrum of emotion regulation skills, and this contributes to the complexity of clinical presentations (Lavender et al., 2015). Additionally, borderline personality disorder (BPD) is the most frequently diagnosed co-occurring personality disorder diagnosis in individuals with anorexia nervosa (AN) and bulimia nervosa (BN) (Chen, Brown, Harned, & Linehan, 2009; Sansone, Levitt, & Sansone, 2004). A diagnosis of BPD presents its own challenges in treatment, and the presence of BPD with an ED may further complicate adherence to empirically supported ED treatments. For example, the presence of co-occurring BN and BPD significantly increases risk for suicidal behavior, even when statistically adjusting for mood, anxiety, and substance use disorders (Reas, Pedersen, Karterud, & Rø, 2015).

Across many disorders, clinicians often report that they believe that manualized, empirically supported treatments will not work with clients with multiple co-occurring conditions (Stirman, DeRubeis, Crits-Christoph, & Brody, 2003; Waller, 2016). This is also the case with clinicians who treat EDs. Some research demonstrates that although clinicians use cognitive-behavioral techniques for their ED patients, they may not use manuals. One of the most commonly cited reasons for this lack of fidelity to manuals from clinicians is that manuals do not address the complexity and comorbidity of a large percentage of their patients (Haas & Clopton, 2003, Thompson-Brenner & Westen, 2005a, 2005b).

DBT and complex ED presentations

Given these challenges, DBT has been explored as a credible alternative to CBT-E for some ED patients (Bankoff, Karpel, Forbes, & Pantalone, 2012). A meta-analysis of 'third wave' treatments (e.g. such as mindfulness based treatments or response focused treatments) indicates that these therapies yielded moderate to large effect sizes in Eating Disorder Examination scores, binge eating and purging symptoms, weight and shape concerns, depression, and self-esteem (Linardon, Fairburn, Fitzsimmons-Craft, Wilfley, & Brennan, 2017). Additionally, these effect sizes were equivalent to CBT for eating disorders (Linardon et al., 2017). Many ED patients may have a variety of life threatening, therapy interfering and quality of life targets, in addition to the ED symptoms, that can be addressed in a DBT framework (Wisniewski, 2016). Additionally, given that therapist burnout and drift from fidelity has been discussed in ED treatment (e.g. Waller, 2016, 2016), the role of the consultation team in a DBT program (Linehan, 1993) is well-suited to help clinicians work effectively with complex ED clients. There have been several adaptations of DBT for the treatment of eating disorders. For example, Federici and Wisniewski (2013) and Wisniewski & Ben-Porath (2015)) have developed an approach to treating multi-diagnostic eating disorders in a comprehensive DBT format (Multi-Diagnostic ED DBT or MED-DBT) (Federici & Wisniewski, 2013, 2015; Wisniewski, 2016; Wisniewski & Ben-Porath, 2015). Several studies demonstrate that DBT is associated with significant reductions in binge eating, purging, NSSI, suicide attempts, hospitalizations, and mood disturbances (e.g. Chen, Matthew, Allen, Kuo, & Linehan, 2008; Safer & Chen, 2016). However, there are very few randomized controlled trials comparing DBT to empirically supported treatments for EDs, such as CBT (but see Chen et al., 2017).

Current paper

Although it is likely that some individuals in published treatment trials for eating disorders engaged in self-injury or had suicidal ideation, data related to these outcomes are typically not reported in RCTs for EDs. Thus, a thorough discussion of referral decision making for patients with Multi-diagnostic EDs (Federici & Wisniewski, 2013) is lacking. Previous researchers have discussed decision making models for treating complex ED presentations, but these typically focus on the chronicity and severity of ED symptoms or ED diagnosis to determine treatment choice (e.g. Dingemans et al., 2017). Fairburn provides some guidance regarding when to address co-morbid diagnoses in ED treatment, but does not address chronic suicidal behavior nor BPD (Fairburn, Cooper, & Waller, 2008). Thus, the decision making model described in this paper was developed as other models do not appear to capture the unique needs of multi-diagnostic complex ED presentations.

Based on treatment outcome research to date, it appears that CBT-E is the most efficacious treatment for eating disorders, and DBT is the treatment of choice for BPD. However, when adults present for treatment for EDs and have multiple co-occurring problems, like self-injury or suicidality, clinicians grapple with difficult questions such as, 'How do I make decisions about which treatment to use'? In this paper, we first describe a DBT based and research informed conceptual model for treatment decision making in an outpatient non-academic setting. We also apply this model to a de-identified case. In this model, we emphasize determining the function of specific symptoms as a way to guide treatment decision making. In order to further illustrate the way that this decision making model is used, we provide descriptive data regarding clients who present to a non-academic setting for treatment of comples/multi-diagnostic EDs and their disposition.

Practice setting and intake procedure

The decision making model described in this paper was developed in an outpatient private practice that uses empirically supported treatments. The practice group consists of several licensed clinical psychologists, licensed clinical social workers, (14 therapy providers total) a nutritionist, a physician's assistant, and a psychiatrist. Therapists have been trained in several empirically supported treatments, including CBT-E, Family Based Treatment (FBT) for AN, DBT, and other evidence based practices such as exposure and response prevention. The DBT consultation team includes the psychiatrist and nutritionist. The practice uses a staged decision making model to inform treatment decisions following initial intake based on treatment outcome research, DBT models of stages of treatment, and available research data on medical risk.

As part of the decision making process, all clients who express interest in treatment at the practice are asked to complete a structured clinical intake interview that assesses a full range of psychiatric diagnoses, trauma history, and BPD. Additionally, information is collected about previous treatment, treatment goals, and age of onset of symptoms. Following the intake interview, a preliminary assignment to treatment is made, based on this information and how it fits into the decision making model described below. The preliminary diagnosis given during the intake interview is confirmed during the first two sessions by the assigned individual provider. Additionally, this time is used to conduct a functional analysis of symptoms, in order to further inform treatment decision making.

Decision tree: to DBT or not to DBT?

Figure 1 presents a flow chart of the decision making model. First, if a client with an eating disorder is diagnosed with BPD following their initial intake, they are referred to DBT. If a client does not have a diagnosis of BPD, the following decision tree steps are used. The remainder of the decision making model is based on a series of behavioral analyses that include the context of the behavior, what happens following the behavior, and the function of the behavior for the client (e.g. functional analysis of the behavior). Stage 1 targets

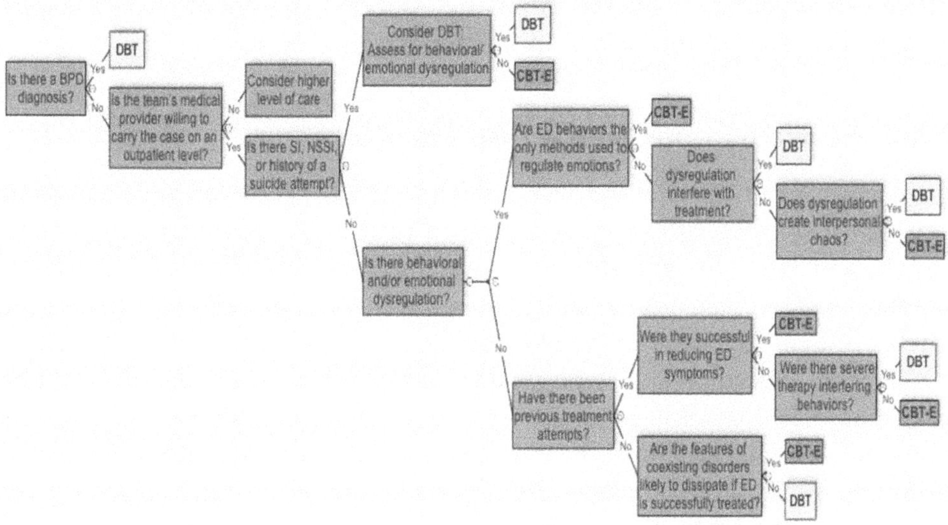

Figure 1. Decision making model for DBT or CBT-E for complex eating disorders.

are assessed. Following DBT protocols, Stage 1 targets are life-threatening behavior, therapy interfering behavior, and quality of life-interfering behavior. Life-threatening behavior may lead to a referral to DBT. In the context of ED clients, assessment of life-threatening behavior is based on structured clinical interviews regarding suicide risk, assessment of NSSI, and medical monitoring with an on staff physician assistant or the patient's primary care physician. Thus, if an ED symptom presents an immediate life-threatening medical risk, this is considered a Stage 1 target for treatment. Note that medical instability itself does not necessarily indicate referral to DBT. Rather, medical instability that is life-threatening, in our model, indicates a referral to DBT. As described previously, many ED patients also have suicidal ideation, behavior, or NSSI. If these are present, our decision making model suggest functional assessment of these behaviors. If these behaviors are functionally related to emotion dysregulation, we suggest DBT. If these behaviors are triggered by ED symptoms, such as restriction or self-weighing, then CBT-E is considered. In other words, if sucidality appears to be secondary to ED symptoms, clients may be referred to CBT-E. Thus far, the only diagnosis (in our model) that warrants a specific treatment disposition is BPD. Recent NSSI or a suicide attempt, for example, may not indicate a referral to DBT, and, conversely, a diagnosis of BN may not indicate a referral to CBT-E. Following this, other quality of life interfering behavior and Stage 2 targets are assessed. Individuals who have emotion dysregulation that interferes with treatment or creates interpersonal chaos are also referred to DBT. Stage 2 targets are typically related to PTSD and shame which interferes with building a life worth living. Individuals without Stage 1 targets are typically referred for CBT-E in our model.

Using the decision tree with a case example

As an example of the decision tree model, a case is presented with course of treatment described. All services described (nutrition, medical management, CBT-E, and DBT are offered at our outpatient private practice). "Anna" is a female who was 36 years old at the time of her first self-referral to our practice. First, the client requested nutrition services and initially described her goals as related to a specific medical condition (a heart condition). She participated in the clinical intake procedure described above. During this interview, she denied ED symptoms, as well as other symptoms of mood disorders, PTSD, and other conditions, including BPD. Thus, she was not initially referred to therapy. However, once enrolled in nutrition services, multiple ED symptoms consistent with a diagnosis of AN, restricting subtype emerged. She terminated services after repeated attempts to engage her in CBT-E for ED symptoms, and began therapy with another provider in the community.

Two years after her initial presentation treatment with our team nutritionist, she again self-referred for therapy at the clinic for depressive symptoms. At the time of this self-referral, she disclosed more information during the clinical intake process than she had in the previous intake. During this second referral intake, she disclosed having previous trauma experiences (i.e., two sexual assaults, emotional and verbal abuse, childhood neglect) and stated that she experienced PTSD symptoms of flashbacks, nightmares, dissociation, sleep disturbance, and feelings of detachment. She also reported depressive symptoms, such as chronic feelings of hopelessness and worthlessness. Additionally, Anna reported emotional dysregulation triggered by fear of abandonment in multiple interpersonal relationships. Anna also reported that her most recent relationship rupture triggered her to cut herself with a knife, for which she was medically hospitalized for five days. She noted she did not follow up with medical care as requested by the dietitian during her initial presentation at the practice. Finally, she continued to minimize ED symptoms.

After this initial telephone intake, it was unclear whether or not a diagnosis of BPD was warranted. The client reported emotion dysregulation, fear of abandonment, and self-injury that were consistent with a diagnosis of BPD. However, Anna also reported significant impairment from PTSD symptoms. Additionally, the severity of her ED symptoms was not clear from this intake, given her history of denial of illness related to ED. Our team's hesitation to initially diagnose with BPD was primarily due to the following issue. As outlined by Fairburn et al. (2008) it was initially unclear whether or not the symptoms consistent with BPD (e.g. mood disturbance) were due to the chronicity of malnutrition and self-starvation, or due to PTSD, as opposed to BPD. Thus, the team needed more information about how much her eating behavior was impacting her emotion dysregulation, and whether and how the PTSD symptoms were functionally related to her emotion dysregulation and self-injury, in order to make a determination for treatment disposition. In short, as it was unclear whether or not a diagnosis of BPD was accurate, she was not immediately referred to DBT following the telephone intake.

Following the telephone intake, Anna had assessment sessions with a therapist. The therapist observed symptoms consistent with an eating disorder diagnosis, similar to those observed by the nutritionist during her first self-referral. These symptoms included low weight (BMI that fluctuated between 17 and 18.5), dietary restriction, and excessive exercise. Due to her medical condition, her eating disorder symptoms were potentially life-threatening. Following these initial assessment sessions, the team determined that Anna had several Stage 1 and Stage 2 targets that indicated a referral to DBT. The Stage 1 targets were NSSI as an emotion regulation tool and potential life-threatening complications from eating disordered behavior, as well as therapy interfering behavior (based on previous treatment experiences), emotion dysregulation, and interpersonal chaos. Stage 2 targets included PTSD symptoms related to childhood trauma and later traumatic events. Throughout therapy, and consistent with this conceptualization, Anna reported an increase in suicidal and NSSI urges and/or behaviors each time she perceived/experienced a rupture in interpersonal relationships (e.g., intimate, friends, professional, family). Following her engagement in comprehensive DBT and further effective assessment(s) of behaviors and functional analysis of behaviors, Anna was given a diagnosis of BPD. Anna's case highlights the usefulness of functional analysis, especially when an initial diagnosis is unclear. For example, she initially minimized the severity of ED symptoms, and it was unclear whether or not PTSD and ED symptoms were triggers for behaviors consistent with BPD. However, the use of the clinical decision making model described led the team to refer her to DBT, despite the uncertainty surrounding the diagnosis.

Clinical data on the decision tree

Next, we describe how the decision making model presented in the paper functions in a clinical practice. We briefly describe the characteristics of individuals referred to comprehensive DBT vs. CBT-E in our outpatient private practice setting. Prior to the data review, we hypothesized that length of illness, specific ED diagnosis, and number of previous treatment attempts would not differentiate individuals with EDs who are referred for DBT as opposed to CBT-E. The development of this hypothesis was based in part on clinical observation, and in part based on our review of the literature on emotion dysregulation in

EDs (Lavender et al., 2015). In general, we hypothesize that the function of the behavior or ED symptom is more clinically relevant for treatment disposition than the diagnosis itself. Additionally, many ED clients do not receive empirically supported treatments for their illness (e.g. Waller, 2016). Thus, we did not assume that multiple prior treatment attempts indicated that a client had engaged in therapy interfering behavior or that CBT-E had failed. Rather, we assumed that it was possible that they had not yet been offered adherent empirically supported ED treatment.

Participants

Participants in the data review were 228 adult clients who presented for treatment of an eating disorder over the past four years. The age range of clients presenting for ED treatment was 18 years to 58 years of age, with a mean age at intake of 27.47 years (sd = 7.86). In this sample, 92.1% identified themselves as women, while 7.9% identified themselves as men. In this group, 19.3% were diagnosed with AN-restricting type; 5.3% with AN-binge/purge type; 13.6% with BN; 7.0% with BED, 48.7% with Otherwise specified feeding and eating disorder (OSFED); 3.5% with psychogenic vomiting; and 2.6% with avoidant restrictive food intake disorder (ARFID). Overall, clients reported a wide range of length of illness, with the onset of the ED ranging from 3 months ago to 552 months. The mean length of illness was 114.94 months (9.57 years). Clients with AN-restricting subtype reported statistically significantly fewer months of illness than all other groups.

Procedures

We reviewed intake data from the 228 adults who presented for ED treatment over a period of four years. As described above, each client completed a structured clinical interview of symptoms, trauma history, treatment history, and demographic information. We then reviewed each client's chart to determine their ultimate treatment disposition. We entered information on the presence vs. absence of suicidal ideation, suicide attempts, NSSI, symptoms of emotional/behavioral dysregulation, length of illness, ED diagnosis, whether or not they had received previous treatment for an ED, and what type of treatment they were referred to at our practice into a data file. We used X^2 tests and independent samples t-tests to compare the characteristics of those referred to DBT vs. CBT-E.

Results

In this group, 78 clients (34.2% of the sample) were referred to comprehensive DBT, while 140 (61.4%) were referred to CBT-E. The remaining 10 clients were referred to another type of evidence-based treatment. There were no statistically significant differences in diagnostic categories in clients referred for DBT vs. CBT-E, nor were there statistically significant differences in age or length of illness. Among clients who were referred to DBT, 46.2% reported NSSI, 41.0% reported at least one past suicide attempt, 64.1% reported suicidal ideation, 64.1% reported emotional or behavioral dysregulation that had been difficult to manage in previous treatments, and 65.4% having reported more than one of these symptoms. A total of 3.8% did not report any of these symptoms, and were referred to DBT due to multiple previous unsuccessful treatment attempts or therapy interfering behavior in another form of treatment.

Among the clients referred to CBT-E, 8.3% reported NSSI, 2.8% reported a past suicide attempt, 15.9% reported suicidal ideation, and 17.1% reported severe behavioral/emotional dysregulation. Finally, among the clients referred for treatment, 65.4% of DBT clients and 57.1% of CBT-E clients reported having had previous treatment for their eating disorder. This difference was not statistically significant ($X^2 = 3.17$, $p < .21$).

In summary, data from this outpatient practice show that adult clients with EDs who present for intakes, regardless of disposition to CBT-E vs. DBT, have a range of diagnoses

(AN, BN, OSFED, BED), have typically had a multi-year course of illness, and have typically tried a range of empirically supported and non-empirically supported treatments in other settings without full symptom remission. The factor that distinguishes treatment disposition is not length of illness or previous treatment attempts or diagnosis. Instead, it was life-threatening behaviors or behaviors related to emotion dysregulation that co-occurred with the ED symptoms. Clients presenting for ED treatment who were referred to comprehensive DBT had some combination of past suicide attempts, suicidal ideation, NSSI, or emotional/behavioral dysregulation, or had significant therapy interfering behaviors in other forms of treatment. Clients who were referred to comprehensive DBT had a range of diagnoses (AN, BN, OSFED, or BED), and no one diagnostic category was more likely than another to be assigned to DBT. Thus, this data demonstrates that, at least in this setting, some of the previously published decision making tools do not capture all the features that clinicians may consider when presented with an individual with a multi-diagnostic ED.

Discussion

Little research has investigated a decision making process regarding when to refer adult ED patients to CBT versus DBT as a first line approach. We suggest a novel way of determining initial treatment by including not only primary diagnosis and chronicity of illness, but also the function of eating disorder behavior. Using this decision making model, a client does not get referred to a specific treatment based solely on their diagnosis (e.g. adult clients with BN do not automatically get referred to CBT-E). Instead, functional analysis of symptoms is the primary assessment method for choosing an initial treatment. We suggest that choosing DBT prior to CBT may be indicated when the function of the ED behaviors is driven by emotion dysregulation. This does not preclude the possibility that ED behaviors may be so life-threatening that a higher level of care is warranted prior to engaging in outpatient treatment. And, empirical tests of treatment matching would further inform the validity of this decision making model. We also reviewed our intake data to describe how the decision making model has been used in a private practice setting. At this time, it was not possible to describe the outcomes of patients who were referred to DBT vs. CBT-E. However, as with the individual case presented, we wished to focus on decision making regarding how to select a treatment plan for multi-diagnostic or complex ED patients when they initially present for treatment.

The case described highlights the benefit of having nutritionists, psychiatrists, and medical providers join the DBT consultation team. Given the interaction between impulsivity and ineffective attempts at emotion regulation, the medical status of complex ED pts can change abruptly. The risk of cardiovascular events or suicide are high in chronic eating disorders (Mehler & Brown, 2015; Mitchell, 2016). If a patient is experiencing an increase in a Stage 1 target behavior (which can happen rapidly) or behavior related to the eating disorder (e.g., increase in binge/purge behaviors, severe restriction, increased laxative use), routine medical management is required. Having a provider who has followed the patient routinely can prevent therapy interfering hospitalizations. It is also worth noting that psychological symptoms caused or worsened by semi-starvation include, but are not limited to, depression, suicidal ideation, labile mood, and compulsive behaviors; thus increasing risk for both medical and emotional stability. A medical provider who understands the DBT model and also believes that frequent hospitalizations are a behavioral target themselves (frequent hospitalizations are a barrier to having a life worth living) is imperative. Thus, it may be most effective for the medical provider to be part of the DBT consultation team. An adaptation to a traditional DBT approach when treating complex eating disorder is to include medication management providers, medical providers, and dietitians on the consultation team, in addition to individual therapists who are working with the eating disorder patient. (Our program has long included these members on our team and found an increased comprehensiveness in assessing and treating the patient, as well as increase cohesion of the team, fidelity to the treatment, and ability to balance at times conflicting clinical demands of each discipline).

Conclusions

The current paper describes a research and DBT informed decision making model for treatment referral. The model was developed as there are not clear cut empirically based guidelines for how to determine the best course of treatment when suicidality/NSSI and medically complex eating disorder symptoms are both present upon initial referral, and both equally important to treat. The questions that prompted the development of this decision making model are clinically relevant and difficult to empirically test. Thus, this decision making model should be empirically tested and client outcome data gathered. Overall, this highlights the "research-practice gap" that presents challenges to researchers and clinicians in the field.

References

Bankoff, S. M., Karpel, M. G., Forbes, H. E., & Pantalone, D. W. (2012). A systematic review of dialectical behavior therapy for the treatment of eating disorders. *Eating Disorders, 20* (3), 196–215. doi:10.1080/10640266.2012.668478

Chen, E. Y., Brown, M. Z., Harned, M. S., & Linehan, M. M. (2009). A comparison of borderline personality disorder with and without eating disorders. *Psychiatry Research, 170* (1), 86–90. doi:10.1016/j.psychres.2009.03.006

Chen, E. Y., Cacioppo, J., Fettich, K., Gallop, R., McCloskey, M. S., Olino, T., & Zeffiro, T. A. (2017). An adaptive randomized trial of dialectical behavior therapy and cognitive behavior therapy for binge-eating. *Psychological Medicine, 47*(4), 703–717. doi:10.1017/S0033291716002543

Chen, E. Y., Matthew, L., Allen, C., Kuo, J. R., & Linehan, M. M. (2008). Dialectical behavior therapy for clients with binge-eating disorder or bulimia nervosa and borderline personality disorder. *International Journal of Eating Disorders, 41*(6), 505–512. doi:10.1002/eat.20522

Dingemans, A. E., Goorden, M., Lötters, F. J., Bouwmans, C., Danner, U. N., van Elburg, A. A., … Hakkaart van Roijen, L. (2017). Development and validation of a decision tool for early identification of adult patients with severe and complex eating disorder psychopathology in need of highly specialized care. *European Eating Disorders Review, 25*(5), 366–372. doi:10.1002/erv.2528

Fairburn, C. G., Cooper, Z., & Waller, D. (2008). Complex cases" and comorbidity. In Fairburn & Cooper (Eds.), *Cognitive behavior therapy and eating disorders* (pp. 245–258). New York, NY: Guilford Press.

Federici, A., & Wisniewski, L. (2013). An intensive DBT program for patients with multidiagnostic eating disorder presentations: A case series analysis. *International Journal of Eating Disorders, 46*(4), 322–331. doi:10.1002/eat.22112

Federici, A., & Wisniewski, L. (2015). Dialectical behavior therapy for clients with complex and multidiagnostic eating disorder presentations. In L. Choate (Ed.), *Eating Disorders and Obesity: A Counselor's Guide to Treatment and Prevention* (pp. 375–397). Alexandria, VA: American Counseling Association.

Haas, H. L., & Clopton, J. R. (2003). Comparing clinical and research treatments for eating disorders. *International Journal of Eating Disorders, 33*(4), 412–420. doi:10.1002/(ISSN)1098-108X

Islam, M. A., Steiger, H., Jimenez-Murcia, S., Israel, M., Granero, R., Aguera, Z., & Fernandez- Aranda, F. (2015). Non-suicidal self-injury in different eating disorder types:

Relevance of personality traits and gender. *European Eating Disorders Review*, *23*(6), 553–560. doi:10.1002/erv.2374

Kostro, K., Lerman, J. B., & Attia, E. (2014). The current status of suicide and self-injury in eating disorders: A narrative review. *Journal of Eating Disorders*, *2*(19), 1–9. doi:10.1186/s40337-014-0019-x

Lavender, J. M., Wonderlich, S. A., Engel, S. G., Gordon, K. H., Kaye, W. H., & Mitchell, J. E. (2015). Dimensions of emotion dysregulation in anorexia nervosa and bulimia nervosa: A conceptual review of the empirical literature. *Clinical Psychology Review*, *40*, 111–122. doi:10.1016/j.cpr.2015.05.010

Linardon, J., Fairburn, C. G., Fitzsimmons-Craft, E. E., Wilfley, D. E., & Brennan, L. (2017). The empirical status of the third-wave behaviour therapies for the treatment of eating disorders: A systematic review. *Clinical Psychology Review*, *58*, 125–140. doi:10.1016/j.cpr.2017.10.005

Linehan, M. M. (1993). *Cognitive-behavioral treatment of borderline personality disorder*. New York, NY: Guilford Publications.

Mehler, P. S., & Brown, C. (2015). Anorexia nervosa–medical complications. *Journal of Eating Disorders*, *3*(1), 11. doi:10.1186/s40337-015-0040-8

Mitchell, J. E. (2016). Medical comorbidity and medical complications associated with binge eating disorder. *International Journal of Eating Disorders*, *49*(3), 319–323. doi:10.1002/eat.22452

Poulsen, S., Lunn, S., Daniel, S. I. F., Folke, S., Mathiesen, B. B., Katznelson, H., & Fairburn, C. G. (2014). A randomized controlled trial of psychoanalytic psychotherapy or cognitive- behavioral therapy for bulimia nervosa. *The American Journal of Psychiatry*, *171*, 109–116. doi:10.1176/appi.ajp.2013.12121511

Reas, D. L., Pedersen, G., Karterud, S., & Rø, Ø. (2015). Self-harm and suicidal behavior in borderline personality disorder with and without bulimia nervosa. *Journal of Consulting and Clinical Psychology*, *83*(3), 643. doi:10.1037/ccp0000014

Safer, D. L., & Chen, E. (2016). Dialectical behavior therapy for binge eating. In A. F. Haynos, E. M. Forman, M. L. Butryn & J. Lillis (Eds.), *Mindfulness and acceptance for treating eating disorders and weight concerns: Evidence-based interventions* (pp. 71). Oakland, CA: NewHarbringer Publications.

Sansone, R. A., Levitt, J. L., & Sansone, L. A. (2004). The prevalence of personality disorders among those with eating disorders. *Eating Disorders*, *13*(1), 7–21. doi:10.1080/10640260590893593

Stirman, S. W., DeRubeis, R. J., Crits-Christoph, P., & Brody, P. E. (2003). Are samples in randomized controlled trials of psychotherapy representative of community outpatients? A new methodology and initial findings. *Journal of Consulting and Clinical Psychology*, *71*(6), 963. doi:10.1037/0022-006X.71.6.963

Thompson-Brenner, H., & Westen, D. (2005a). A naturalistic study of psychotherapy for bulimia nervosa, part 1: Comorbidity and therapeutic outcome. *The Journal of Nervous and Mental Disease*, *193*(9), 573–584. doi:10.1097/01.nmd.0000178843.81100.eb

Thompson-Brenner, H., & Westen, D. (2005b). A naturalistic study of psychotherapy for bulimia nervosa, Part 2: Therapeutic interventions in the community. *The Journal of Nervous and Mental Disease*, *193*(9), 585–595. doi:10.1097/01.nmd.0000178883.82580.18

Waller, G. (2016). Treatment protocols for eating disorders: Clinicians' attitudes, concerns, adherence and difficulties delivering evidence-based psychological interventions. *Current Psychiatry Reports*, *18*(4), 36. doi:10.1007/s11920-016-0679-0

Wisniewski, L. (2016). *Addressing self-injury and therapy-interfering behaviors in eating disorder treatment across the developmental spectrum: A DBT approach* [PowerPoint Presentation]. Retrieved from The Emily Program.

Wisniewski, L., & Ben-Porath, D. D. (2015). Dialectical behavior therapy and eating disorders: The use of contingency management procedures to manage dialectical dilemmas. *American Journal of Psychotherapy*, *69*(2), 129–140. doi:10.1176/appi.psychotherapy.2015.69.2.129

Wonderlich, S. A., Peterson, C. B., Crosby, R. D., Smith, T. L., Klein, M. H., Mitchell, J. E., & Crow, S. J. (2014). A randomized controlled comparison of integrative cognitive- affective therapy (ICAT) and enhanced cognitive-behavioral therapy (CBT-E) for bulimia nervosa. *Psychological Medicine*, *44*(3), 543–553. doi:10.1017/S0033291713001098

Acceptance-based skill acquisition and cognitive reappraisal in a culturally responsive treatment for binge eating in adolescence

Rebecca C. Kamody, Idia B. Thurston, and E. Thomaseo Burton

ABSTRACT

Emotional overeating, or eating in excess to soothe negative emotions, is a high-risk behavior for the future development of the binge-eating disorder (BED). The Emotional Overeating Intervention (EOI) is a culturally responsive, 10-week condensed dialectical behavior therapy (DBT) skills group intervention for adolescents endorsing emotional-overeating and binge-eating behaviors. The present study served as a secondary analysis of the intervention data, with the aim of using quantitative measures and qualitative interviews to examine intervention acceptability and DBT skill acquisition. Data were analyzed using descriptive statistics for quantitative surveys and qualitative content analysis for interviews. Among the 15 adolescents (M_{age} = 15.40 years; 73.3% identifying as female; 100% identifying as Black) who participated in the EOI pilot trial, most identified learning acceptance-based DBT skills, particularly radical acceptance, as both highly acceptable and the most useful aspect of treatment. Participants reported increases in distress tolerance appraisal and emotion regulation cognitive reappraisal scale scores from baseline to post-intervention. Accordingly, acceptance-based DBT skills may be associated with change-based cognitive strategies, which may contribute to improvements in emerging BED pathology. Findings serve as an initial step in informing preventative models of scalable interventions for subthreshold BED among adolescents, by identifying variables that warrant investigation as potential mechanisms of change.

Clinical implications

- Using a mixed-methods approach, participants enrolled in a DBT-informed skills intervention for binge-eating behaviors reported on their skill acquisition and acceptability of skills.

- Participants' self-report indicated that both their change-based emotion regulation cognitive reappraisal and acceptance-based distress tolerance appraisal increased over the course of the emotional overeating intervention.
- Via qualitative and quantitative measures, participants indicated that radical acceptance was the most helpful skill learned to assist with controlling their emotional-overeating behaviors.
- Taken together, the act of turning one's mind to accept the reality of one's circumstances (i.e., radical acceptance), may serve as both an acceptance-based and change-based strategy, to assist with the reappraisal of emotions and decrease emotional overeating.
- The incorporation of traditional change-based reappraisal strategies with acceptance-based appraisal strategies may serve as salient targets in streamlined DBT-informed interventions for the prevention of binge eating among youth.

Binge-eating disorder (BED), typified by eating large quantities of food in a discrete period of time with an accompanying sense of loss of control, is the most common eating disorder with lifetime prevalence rates exceeding those of anorexia nervosa and bulimia nervosa (Hudson, Hiripi, Pope, & Kessler, 2007; Udo & Grilo, 2018). Typical onset of BED is during adolescence, and research suggests that 2.5% of adolescents experience binge-eating symptoms (Swanson, Crow, Le Grange, Swendsen, & Merikangas, 2011). Adolescence is a developmental period in which the risk for emotional and behavioral problems is heightened (Hou et al., 2013; Zhu et al., 2016). Emotional overeating, which involves excessive eating in response to emotional triggers, often begins in adolescence and progresses in severity as stressors increase in adulthood (Hilbert, 2013; Masheb & Grilo, 2006; Tanofsky-Kraff et al., 2007). In fact, perceived stress among adolescents has been shown to increase emotional eating (Nguyen-Rodriguez, Chou, Unger, & Spruijt-Metz, 2008). Youth engaging in subthreshold binge-eating behaviors are still susceptible to physical, social, and psychological sequelae associated with a diagnosis of BED (Field et al., 2012; Trace et al., 2012). For example, researchers have reported associations between loss-of-control eating with increased depressive symptoms and emotional distress (Goldschmidt et al., 2015; Sonneville et al., 2013), as well as excessive weight gain among youth (Tanofsky-Kraff et al., 2011).

Dialectical behavior therapy for disordered eating

With deep roots in the affect regulation model, dialectical behavior therapy (DBT; Linehan, 1993a, 1993b) is an ideal intervention for addressing emotion dysregulation, as is seen in many disordered eating presentations (Bankoff, Karpel, Forbes, & Pantalone, 2012; Lenz, Taylor, Fleming, & Serman, 2014; Linehan & Chen, 2005; Safer, Telch, & Chen, 2009; Wisniewski & Kelly, 2003). Literature supporting the use of DBT as an effective intervention for the treatment of eating disorders (including BED) among youth continues to grow (Fischer & Peterson, 2015; Kamody, Thurston, Pluhar, Han, & Burton, 2019; Pennell, Webb, Agar, Federici, & Couturier, 2019; Peterson, Van Diest, Mara, & Matthews, 2019). However, this vein of scholarship has mostly focused on the use of comprehensive DBT to treat individuals with full criteria eating disorders (Fischer & Peterson, 2015; Safer, Lock, & Couturier, 2007; Salbach-Andrae, Bohnekamp, Pfeiffer, Lehmkuhl, & Miller, 2008). This comprehensive approach, while empirically supported for youth with clinical presentations, may not be warranted for youth with subthreshold BED presentations. Further, the integration of DBT skills with other therapies has demonstrated efficacy among adolescents being treated for a variety of eating disorders (Accurso, Astrachan-Fletcher, O'Brien, McClanahan, & Le Grange, 2018; Anderson et al., 2015; Murray et al., 2015; Pennell et al., 2019) and the use of a condensed, DBT skills *only* intervention for subthreshold BED symptoms has demonstrated promise at reducing binge-eating behaviors among adolescents (Kamody et al., 2019). This is encouraging, considering that research in the prevention of eating disorders indicates that early intervention is associated with greater symptom improvement and more positive long-term outcomes (McClelland et al., 2018).

Culturally-adapting intervention

Research has highlighted potential cultural differences that may influence clinical presentation (Lee-Winn, Reinblatt, Mojtabai, & Mendelson, 2016; Marques et al., 2011), and emphasize the importance of targeted interventions for populations not meeting standard diagnostic thresholds. It is important to utilize diverse and representative samples in intervention adaptation, in order to adapt evidence-based treatments to the patients being targeted (Nock, Goldman, Wang, & Albano, 2004). Research indicates comparable rates of BED among White, Black, and Hispanic racial/ethnic groups within the US, yet higher prevalence of engagement in objective binge episodes for people of color (Marques et al., 2011). This suggests the importance of culturally-adapting interventions for these target populations (Barrera, Castro, Strycker, & Toobert, 2013; Castro, Barrera, & Martinez, 2004).

Due to cultural differences in eating behaviors and body image ideals, the restraint model underlying treatments for BED may not be a culturally appropriate conceptualization of what drives emotional overeating and binge-eating behaviors for all racial/ethnic populations (Taylor, Caldwell, Baser, Faison, & Jackson, 2007). For example, stressors and life experiences have been found to be a more apt explanation of what contributes to disordered eating behaviors among Black women (Taylor et al., 2007), further supporting the affect regulation model as a culturally responsive conceptualization of emotional overeating (i.e., using overeating as a means to cope with stressors or negative emotions; Safer et al., 2009). This conceptualization provides support for the use of a DBT approach, with its underlying theory of the affect regulation model. As adapting DBT for adolescents with binge-eating and emotional-overeating behaviors is a novel area of study, extant research exploring culturally responsive adaptations for this population is limited. It is also worth noting that of the work that has been conducted in DBT for adolescents with eating disorders, participant samples have been predominantly White female youth (Fischer & Peterson, 2015; Salbach-Andrae et al., 2008).

Cognitive reappraisal and disordered eating

Binge-eating behaviors have been associated with negative mood and increased difficulty tolerating distress (Ivanova et al., 2015; Masheb & Grilo, 2006). As such, interventions that bolster adaptive emotion regulation strategies to modulate internal experiences may be a salient approach to address emotional eating and prevent the development of BED. According to the affect regulation model (Telch, Agras, & Linehan, 2001), binge eating is thought to relieve negative emotion, which actually serves to reinforce the binge-eating behavior (Polivy & Herman, 1993). Adaptive emotion regulation strategies, such as cognitive reappraisal (i.e., changing the way one interprets an event in order to alter their emotional response to that event; Gross, 1998), have been found to ameliorate severity of eating disorder pathology, particularly for presentations that include loss-of-control eating behaviors (Aldao & Nolen-Hoeksema, 2010; Danner, Evers, Stok, van Elburg, & de Ridder, 2012). To date, much of the research in cognitive reappraisal strategies and eating are focused on the reappraisal of food craving and not emotions, although the latter may influence eating behaviors (Giuliani & Pfeifer, 2015). It would stand to reason that increases in cognitive reappraisal related to emotion regulation strategies may lead to decreases in emotionally driven overeating behaviors (and subsequently both subthreshold and full threshold BED behaviors). Cognitive reappraisal of emotions, which may underlie interventions applying emotion regulation strategies to disordered eating behaviors (e.g., DBT), however, remains understudied.

Current study

Using a mixed-methods approach, the present study examined specific skill acquisition that occurred during the pilot trial of a culturally responsive, DBT-informed skills intervention for both emotional overeating and binge-eating behaviors. We hypothesized that the intervention would result in gains in cognitive reappraisal strategies, as observed through the acquisition of both acceptance- and change-based skills. We posited that cognitive reappraisal may serve as a potential mechanism influencing treatment outcomes.

Materials and methods

The present study was conducted in three pediatric outpatient clinics co-located within an academic medical center in the Mid-South United States. Over a period of 3 months, all scheduled patients between the ages of 14–18 years were screened for endorsement of emotional-overeating behaviors. Upon check-in for their appointment, youth received a screener with items corresponding to DSM-5 criteria for BED in a yes/no format. All patients endorsing at least one item were contacted by study personnel to assess interest and appropriateness for the *Emotional Overeating Intervention* (EOI). Screening and recruitment began after obtaining Institutional Review Board approval from the University of Tennessee Health Science Center. Exclusion criteria included a formal diagnosis of Intellectual Disability (i.e., IQ < 70) and lack of parent consent.

Intervention

EOI is an adapted DBT skills-based group intervention for adolescents endorsing emotional-overeating behaviors (Pluhar, Kamody, Sanchez, Thurston, & Burton, 2018). The intervention was adapted to be responsive to a number of aspects of the target participants' cultural identities, including race/ethnicity, socioeconomic/class status, developmental age, and gender (with the notable inclusion of male participants). Culturally responsive considerations began with the selection of the theoretical model (i.e., affect regulation model underlying DBT being responsive to racial minority populations) and group-based DBT skills format (particularly important for adolescent socialization and validation of stigmatizing behaviors). Specific adaptations pertained to both session structure and session content. With regard to session structure, the DBT for adolescents skills curriculum was condensed to 10 weeks, and all skills were presented in the context of emotional-overeating behaviors. In addition, skill lessons were all taught within a 1 hour session, during flexible meeting times (evenings and weekends), responsive to busy working parent work schedules and noted barriers to transportation. Skills sessions entailed brief lectures that were reinforced with experiential activities. Lectures included brief multi-media presentations that included visual images and cultural references identifiable to youth from a wide range of racial and ethnic backgrounds (these images and references can be changed to make content more relevant for a particular audience), with non-stigmatizing images of both males and female adolescents included.

In addition, distress tolerance skills were introduced first (prior to mindfulness) so that in-the-moment crisis skills, which could be used immediately to resist emotional overeating urges, were provided early to ensure buy-in and reduce the high dropout often observed within pediatric weight-related interventions (Skelton & Beech, 2011). The pilot trial supported the feasibility and preliminary effectiveness of EOI at reducing binge eating and emotional overeating (Kamody et al., 2019), based on the Eating Disorder Examination Questionnaire (Fairburn & Beglin, 1994) and Emotional Eating Scale for Children and Adolescents (Tanofsky-Kraff et al., 2007; for detailed description of the intervention and special session details, please see Pluhar et al., 2018).

Five cycles of EOI were implemented, with a total of 30 participants completing baseline assessments. Of these, 15 participants completed the full intervention. This 50% attrition rate is consistent with research in pediatric weight-management interventions (upwards of 73%; Skelton & Beech, 2011). The present study sample included only the 15 intervention completers (demographics provided in Table 1), an adequate sample size to achieve saturation (Malterud, Siersma, & Guassora, 2015). No significant differences were found in demographic characteristics between completers and non-completers. Demographic characteristics of the full baseline sample (N = 30) including non-completers, and statistical differences between these groups, can be found in Kamody et al., (2019). The present study served as a secondary analysis of the intervention data.

Measures

Demographic characteristics and anthropometric measures were collected from all participants during intake. Body mass index (BMI; kg/m^2) was calculated using height and weight measurements assessed by trained study

Table 1. Demographic characteristics of intervention completers (N = 15).

	M (SD)
Body Mass Index Z-Score	2.36 (0.62)
Objective Binge Episodes (Self-Report)	3.67 (4.95)
Age	15.40 (1.30)
	N (%)
Gender	–
Male	4 (26.7%)
Female	11 (73.3%)
Race	–
African American/Black	15 (100.0%)
Ethnicity	–
Non-Hispanic	15 (100.0%)
Caregiver Annual Income	–
<$5,000	1 (6.7%)
$5,000-$30,000	3 (20.0%)
$30,001-$50,000	5 (33.3%)
$50,001-$100,000	5 (33.3%)
>$100,000	1 (6.7%)

Note. Objective binge episodes calculated using the Eating Disorder Examination Questionnaire (Fairburn & Beglin, 1994).

personnel, and standardized by age and sex (Kuczmarski et al., 2002). In addition to the measures detailed below, comorbid mental health concerns were assessed using the 113-item parent-report Child Behavior Checklist and 112-item Youth Self-Report (Achenbach, 2009). Individual items (e.g., 'I deliberately try to hurt or kill myself', 'I think about killing myself') were used to assess for safety among all participants.

Distress tolerance scale (DTS)

The DTS is a 15-item self-report measure assessing emotional distress tolerance. Participants were presented with statements regarding feelings of distress, and responded via a 5-point Likert-type scale (5 = *Strongly Disagree* through 1 = *Strongly Agree*). Higher scores are indicative of greater distress tolerance (Simons & Gaher, 2005). The DTS has a single higher-order factor of distress tolerance, comprised of four first-order factor subscales: *Tolerance, Appraisal, Absorption, Regulation*, and demonstrated overall good internal consistency in the present sample (α = 0.83).

Emotion regulation questionnaire for children and adolescents (ERQ-CA)

The ERQ-CA is a 10-item measure of both *cognitive reappraisal* and *expressive suppression* emotion regulation strategies. Participants were presented with items related to emotion regulation, and rated on a 5-point Likert-type scale how much they agreed with each item (1 = *Strongly Disagree* through 5 = *Strongly Agree*). The ERQ-CA is developmentally appropriate for children and adolescents ages 10–18 (Gullone & Taffe, 2012), with higher scores on each subscale representing greater use of that emotion regulation strategy. In the present sample, the ERQ-CA demonstrated acceptable internal consistency (α = 0.80).

DBT skill rating scale (DBT-SRS)

Participants completed the DBT-SRS, developed as part of the evaluation of EOI, to assess acceptability of the various DBT skills taught through the intervention. Participants were provided a list of skills learned over the course of the intervention, and asked to rate the helpfulness of each treatment component on a 5-point Likert-type scale. Ratings of helpfulness ranged from *Not at all Helpful* (1) to *Extremely Helpful* (5).

Interviews

Semi-structured interviews lasting between 15 and 30 minutes were conducted at the last intervention session to assess participants' perception and acceptability of the intervention. Interviews focused on impressions of the session content and the overall intervention structure.

Analytic plan

Given the small size of the pilot trial, quantitative analyses involved the use of descriptive statistical analyses by examining mean changes in skill acquisition from baseline to post-intervention and calculating effect sizes. This approach is aligned with the recommendation to avoid the use of inferential statistics and *p* value hypothesis testing for analyses of small pilot trials in clinical research (Leon, Davis, & Kraemer, 2011). Mean values were also calculated for the DBT-SRS to examine the acceptability of specific skills.

Interviews were transcribed verbatim using an external, HIPAA compliant and confidential transcription service. Exit interviews underwent qualitative content analysis (Hsieh & Shannon, 2005) to identify responses to intervention content and skills acquisition. Specifically, transcripts were reviewed by study personnel, and coding categories were derived from the text data detailing response to structured interview questions, in consensus with the research team (both lead and senior author). Common categories that emerged were used to subsequently code responses for all interviews, and frequencies of response were then calculated. For questions that interviewers omitted, responses were coded as missing. Via content analysis, the codes that emerged were used to understand the most frequently used skills, and potential mechanisms underlying these skills, detailed below.

Results

Within the present sample, all participants identified as Black. Based on self-report measures, small effect sizes were found for mean skill acquisition on two scales assessing aspects of cognitive reappraisal strategies: DTS Appraisal Scale ($d = 0.23$) and ERQ-CA Cognitive Reappraisal Scale ($d = 0.38$). While the post-intervention DTS Appraisal Scale scores continued to be lower than the norm values for this scale (*M* range = 3.52–3.99; Simons & Gaher, 2005), the post-intervention ERQ-CA Cognitive Reappraisal Scale scores were consistent with the norm values for the scale ($M = 21.53$; Gullone & Taffe, 2012). All changes in additional skill acquisition from baseline to post-intervention are provided in Table 2. When rating the helpfulness of each skill using the DBT-SRS, radical acceptance had the highest mean rating (see Table 3).

Based on qualitative data, learning specific DBT skills emerged as the most prevalent response when participants reported on the most useful aspect of the program. The most common response for suggestions to increase enrollment was to advertise to teens how helpful DBT skills are for managing eating behaviors. When asked close-ended questions about the most helpful skill learned, radical acceptance was identified most frequently (see Table 4). A few sample interview quotes supporting the acceptability of learning DBT

Table 2. DBT skill acquisition from baseline to post-intervention.

Measures	Baseline	Post Intervention	Effect Size (Cohen's *d*)
Distress Tolerance Scale (DTS) Total Score	2.06 (0.80)	2.16 (0.90)	0.12
DTS Tolerance Scale	1.84 (0.88)	2.00 (1.02)	0.17
DTS Absorption Scale	1.87 (0.98)	1.98 (1.21)	0.13
DTS Appraisal Scale	1.99 (0.55)	2.14 (0.72)	0.23
DTS Regulation Scale	2.53 (1.28)	2.53 (1.52)	0.00
Emotion Regulation Questionnaire for Children and Adolescents (ERQ-CA) Total	29.80 (7.49)	30.93 (7.75)	0.15
ERQ-CA Cognitive Reappraisal	19.20 (5.87)	21.33 (5.37)	0.38
ERQ-CA Expressive Suppression	10.60 (3.27)	9.60 (4.19)	0.27

Note. Absolute values were calculated for mean changes, and mean changes and effect sizes presented with positive values indicative of improvement in functioning, and negative values indicative of decline in functioning.

Table 3. Acceptability of skills based on DBT skill rating scale.

Treatment Component	Mean (SD)
Self-Soothing	4.60 (0.74)
Radical Acceptance	4.67 (0.62)
'What' and 'How' of Mindfulness	4.60 (0.51)
Mindful Eating	4.63 (0.46)
Three Mind States	4.63 (0.59)
Wise Mind ACCEPTS*	4.20 (0.94)
Riding the Wave	3.80 (1.37)
Opposite Action	4.47 (0.92)
DEAR MAN**	4.47 (0.92)
GIVE†	4.07 (1.10)
FAST††	4.13 (0.99)

Note. 1 = Not at all Helpful; 2 = Slightly Helpful; 3 = Somewhat Helpful; 4 = Very Helpful; 5 = Extremely Helpful.
*ACCEPTS—distress tolerance skill used to distract from difficult situations or emotions (Activities, Contributing, Comparisons, Emotions, Pushing away, Thoughts, Sensations).
**DEAR MAN—interpersonal effectiveness skill aimed to assist in effectively getting needs met in a healthy and productive manner (Describe, Express, Assert, Reinforce, Mindful, Appear confident, Negotiate).
†GIVE—interpersonal effectiveness skill aimed to maintain relationships (be Gentle, act Interested, Validate, use an Easy manner).
††FAST—interpersonal effectiveness skill used to maintain self-respect (Fair, no-Apologies, Stick to values, Truthful).

skills, and the identification of both acceptance- and change-based strategies to decrease binge-eating behaviors include:

> [The most useful part of the program was] "just learning all the different skills, so I could see why I was doing things I was doing, and how I could stop it."
>
> -17yo Black female

> Most useful would be some of the skills we learned about, like, just controlling of your eating and stuff like that, and controlling your emotions when it comes to eating.
>
> -15 yo Black male

> I think radical acceptance was really needed, because you just need to think like … 'Okay, it's [a situation when there is] nothing that I can do anything about, so

Table 4. Emergent themes of structured exit interviews.

	N (%)
Most useful part of the program	
Learning DBT skills	13 (86.7%)
Validation of being with peers with binge-eating behaviors	1 (6.7%)
All aspects	1 (6.7%)
How to encourage other teens to participate	
Advertise how helpful DBT skills are for overeating	4 (26.7%)
Advertise the fun and safe environment	3 (20.0%)
Additional use of gift cards and/or money	2 (13.3%)
Advertise using commercials or flyers	1 (6.7%)
Have former group members co-facilitate future groups	1 (6.7%)
Add more lessons	1 (6.7%)
Nothing (personal decision to attend/not attend)	3 (20.0%)
Most helpful skill learned	
Radical Acceptance	4 (26.7%)
Mindful Eating	2 (13.3%)
Mindfulness	2 (13.3%)
Riding the Wave	2 (13.3%)
Interpersonal Effectiveness (specifically DEAR MAN)	2 (13.3%)
Opposite Action	1 (6.7%)
Wise Mind/States of Mind	1 (6.7%)
Missing (not assessed in interview)	1 (6.7%)

> I might as well just accept it. Thinking about what we learned makes me calm down and relax.
>
> -15yo Black female

> I've used radical acceptance after I've overeaten to help calm myself down. Then afterwards I've used self soothe when I feel like overeating and then I ride the wave.
>
> -14yo Black female

> [The most helpful skill was] "radical acceptance—accepting things that I really didn't want to accept. It was important because I wanted to learn how to accept the fact of what [other] people do. Sometimes you can't change how people act or what they do so it's helpful to maybe accept it and move on, kind of thing, instead of eating".
>
> -16yo Black male

Discussion

The present study served as secondary analyses of intervention data from a pilot trial of a DBT-informed intervention for both emotional overeating and binge-eating behaviors in adolescents, in which we examined skill acquisition that occurred over the intervention course. Participants reported increases in their cognitive reappraisal strategies, both pertaining to change-based emotion regulation, as well as acceptance-based distress tolerance appraisal. In addition, participants found the intervention acceptable, and found the acquisition of acceptance-based DBT skills, such as radical acceptance, to be most helpful. These findings begin to shed light on the aspects of treatment that may have contributed to the improvements observed in the intervention pilot trial, which demonstrated decreases in self-report and caregiver report of both emotional eating and objective binge episodes (Kamody et al., 2019).

It is important for research to not only explore the efficacy of comprehensive treatments for BED, such as DBT, but also to identify more streamlined adaptations for high-risk behaviors and subthreshold presentations. Further, identifying the most salient targets among these interventions, in order to begin to conceptualize potential mechanisms of change, is necessary. This may enhance the dissemination of preventative models with the least burden to both providers and patients, in order to increase uptake of DBT-informed interventions. Identification of skills that may have the greatest impact on subthreshold BED symptoms in youth may help inform less-intensive, possibly even single-session skill interventions, which hold promise for dissemination in alternative settings (e.g., primary and tertiary care). Single-session interventions have evidenced support with other child psychiatric presentations as preventative approaches (Schleider & Weisz, 2018), and may be valuable approaches to targeting subthreshold BED among youth.

Based on the findings of the present study, one mechanism that may contribute to skill acquisition and subsequently decrease BED symptoms, is cognitive reappraisal. Cognitive reappraisal has been examined extensively in the literature as it relates to regulating food intake (Stice et al., 2015; Yokum & Stice, 2013); however, the predominant focus has been on food cravings. When considering developmental level, differences between changes in the cognitive reappraisal of emotions as compared to the reappraisal of food cravings, have been observed among adolescents (Giuliani & Pfeifer, 2015). This suggests that the cognitive reappraisal of emotions, as opposed to craving, may be a distinct construct all together, requiring greater understanding and future research.

Though identified as an acceptance-based distress tolerance skill, trends observed in the present study suggest that learning radical acceptance may impact the change-based emotion regulation strategy of cognitive reappraisal, as it involves turning one's mind to accept the reality of the circumstances of one's environment. The dual nature of this skill, to incorporate an acceptance-based approach to facilitate change-based emotion regulation strategies, may in part account for its high acceptability among participants. Further, this may explain the mixed findings related to emotion regulation acquisition in DBT interventions for youth, as prior research has not found consistent decreases in emotion dysregulation difficulties in such interventions, even when improvements to eating disorder symptoms occur (Murray et al., 2015).

Critical to consider with regard to the findings pertaining to radical acceptance is the importance that this skill may serve for youth with minority identities and/or from underrepresented backgrounds. Indeed, as a skill focused on accepting the reality of one's situation, it would make sense that this distress tolerance may be particularly useful for youth who experience significant life stressors and/or circumstances that may be out of their control (Burton, Kamody, Pluhar, Gray, & Abdullah, 2020), such as those pertaining to the minority stress experience (Sellers, Caldwell, Schmeelk-Cone, & Zimmerman, 2003). Given frustrations with these circumstances, it would stand to reason that maladaptive forms of coping, such as emotional overeating, may result from turning to food for comfort as a primary coping strategy. Thus, it is important to consider these findings in the context of the potential stressors experienced by this sample. Just as important to note, however, is that this theoretical conceptualization is largely speculative, given that experiences with adversity were not assessed in the present study.

Limitations and future directions

Despite the improvements with regard to disordered eating behaviors previously reported for the EOI (Kamody et al., 2019), the present study suggests only small to minimal DBT skill acquisition through the intervention based on participant self-report measures. One explanation for the discrepancy between change in behavioral outcomes and the minimal-reported skill acquisition may be that the constructs facilitating these changes are not accurately assessed by measures used. Similar DBT skills-based interventions with youth with behavioral concerns (Memel, 2012; Nelson-Gray et al., 2006; Ricard, Lerma, & Heard, 2013; Zapolski & Smith, 2017), and with adults with BED symptomatology (Erb, Farmer, & Mehlenbeck, 2013) focus outcomes mainly on primary aims (e.g., decreases in disordered eating, improvements to behavioral outcomes). As such, skill acquisition is often not reported, and thus it is difficult to place these findings in the context of other studies. Based on qualitative responses, participants did report that DBT skill acquisition occurred.

Given this discrepancy, a potential limitation of the present study is that the skill acquisition measures used may not accurately capture these changes for the population of focus. Alternatively, youth may have responded in a socially desirable manner, though the present study sought to address this by having those who conducted exit interviewers to be different study personnel from those who facilitated participants' groups (i.e., facilitators and co-facilitators of other group cycles completing exit interviews). Nevertheless, these limitations highlight the utility of mixed-methods approaches when evaluating intervention implementation and acceptability. Future research should attempt to replicate these findings with additional and alternative objective measures of skill acquisition. One avenue to be explored by future research in order to address this limitation would be the use of validated measures of DBT skills use, such as the DBT Ways of Coping Checklist (Neacsiu, Rizvi, Vitaliano, Lynch, & Linehan, 2010).

Another notable limitation of the present study is the inability to specify why the skills identified as helpful by participants, were indeed the most helpful to them. While qualitative interviews did prompt participants to explain 'why' when identifying the skills (such as with the anecdotal responses provided above from participants), session-level data were not gathered to qualify how exactly participants implemented these skills. This will be an important focus of future research, to better understand the potential mechanisms facilitating the benefits of specific skills.

Although recruitment was not limited based on identified racial/ethnic background, recruitment occurred in a naturalistic setting in which Black individuals represented the majority of the treatment population. Thus, while the all Black sample allowed for the examination of how the affect regulation model may be most appropriate for Black adolescents (as was hypothesized), generalizability of findings to other racial and ethnic groups may be limited. Finally, the small sample size of the present study is a limitation of the study. While the present sample was adequate to reach saturation for the qualitative analyses (Malterud et al., 2015), the small *N* limits the generalizability and interpretability of the quantitative findings.

Conclusion

Given the focus of the present study on identifying potential mechanisms of change reported by participants within this intervention, these findings provide an important first step to inform research aiming to identify potential mechanisms of change in DBT-informed BED treatments. Future research should continue to build upon these findings, with the use of larger samples to evaluate the impact of radical acceptance and the role of cognitive reappraisal, as salient targets for acceptance- and change-based strategies in youth with emotional overeating and binge-eating behaviors. Once able to identify these mechanisms more definitively, the development of brief, scalable interventions using optimal skills for emotional overeating in diverse settings may be more attainable to prevent BED in adolescence.

Acknowledgments

We would like to acknowledge Kristina Decker, M.A., Robin Hardin, M.A., Caroline Kaufman, M.S., Courtney Maclin-Akinyemi, M.S., and Tiffany Rybak, Ph.D., for serving as DBT skills group facilitators and co-facilitators for the present research intervention.

Declaration of interest statement

The authors have no conflicts of interest to disclose.

Funding

This work was supported by an International Society for the Improvement and Teaching of Dialectical Behavior Therapy Student Research Grant; a Children's Foundation Research Institute at Le Bonheur Children's Hospital Research Grant, and the Brinkley Foundation. Funding sources played no role in study design, conduct of research, or preparation of this manuscript.

ORCID

Rebecca C. Kamody http://orcid.org/0000-0002-3307-8117
Idia B. Thurston http://orcid.org/0000-0003-2484-2985
E. Thomaseo Burton http://orcid.org/0000-0002-7772-6235

References

Accurso, E. C., Astrachan-Fletcher, E., O'Brien, S., McClanahan, S. F., & Le Grange, D. (2018). Adaptation and implementation of family-based treatment enhanced with dialectical behavior therapy skills for anorexia nervosa in community-based specialist clinics. *Eating Disorders: the Journal of Treatment & Prevention*, *26*, 149–163. doi:10.1080/10640266.2017.1330319

Achenbach, T. M. (2009). *The Achenbach system of empirically based assessment (ASEBA): Development, findings, theory, and applications*. Burlington: University of Vermont Research Center for Children, Youth, & Famlies.

Aldao, A., & Nolen-Hoeksema, S. (2010). Specificity of cognitive emotion regulation strategies: A transdiagnostic examination. *Behaviour Research and Therapy*, *48*, 974–983. doi:10.1016/j.brat.2010.06.002

Anderson, L. K., Murray, S. B., Ramirez, A. L., Rockwell, R., Le Grange, D., & Kaye, W. H. (2015). The integration of family-based treatment and dialectical behavior therapy for adolescent bulimia nervosa: Philosophical and practical considerations. *Eating Disorders: the Journal of Treatment & Prevention*, *23*, 325–335. doi:10.1080/10640266.2015.1042319

Bankoff, S. M., Karpel, M. G., Forbes, H. E., & Pantalone, D. W. (2012). A systematic review of dialectical behavior therapy for the treatment of eating disorders. *Eating Disorders: the Journal of Treatment & Prevention*, *20*, 196–215. doi:10.1080/10640266.2012.668478

Barrera, M., Jr., Castro, F. G., Strycker, L. A., & Toobert, D. J. (2013). Cultural adaptations of behavioral health interventions: A progress report. *Journal of Consulting and Clinical Psychology*, *81*, 196–205. doi:10.1037/a0027085

Burton, E. T., Kamody, R. C., Pluhar, E. I., Gray, E., & Abdullah, S. (2020). Radical acceptance and obesity-related health conditions: A case report. *Journal of Clinical Psychology in Medical Settings*, Epub Ahead of Print. doi:10.1007/s10880-019-09696-2

Castro, F. G., Barrera, M., Jr., & Martinez, C. R., Jr. (2004). The cultural adaptation of prevention interventions: Resolving tensions between fidelity and fit. *Prevention Science*, *5*, 41–45. doi:10.1023/B:PREV.0000013980.12412.cd

Danner, U. N., Evers, C., Stok, F. M., van Elburg, A. A., & de Ridder, D. T. D. (2012). A double burden: Emotional eating and lack of cognitive reappraisal in eating disordered women. *European Eating Disorders Review*, *20*, 490–495. doi:10.1002/erv.2184

Erb, S., Farmer, A., & Mehlenbeck, R. (2013). A condensed dialectical behavior therapy skills group for binge eating disorder: Overcoming winter challenges. *Journal of Cognitive Psychotherapy*, *27*, 338–358. doi:10.1891/0889-8391.27.4.338

Fairburn, C. G., & Beglin, S. J. (1994). Assessment of eating disorders: Interview or self-report questionnaire?. *International Journal of Eating Disorders, 16*, 363–370. doi:10.1002/1098-108X(199412)16:4<363::AID-EAT2260160405>3.0.CO;2-#

Field, A. E., Sonneville, K. R., Micali, N., Crosby, R. D., Swanson, S. A., Laird, N. M., ... Horton, N. J. (2012). Prospective association of common eating disorders and adverse outcomes. *Pediatrics, 130*, e289–e295. doi:10.1542/peds.2011-3663

Fischer, S., & Peterson, C. (2015). Dialectical behavior therapy for adolescent binge eating, purging, suicidal behavior, and non-suicidal self-injury: A pilot study. *Psychotherapy, 52*, 78–92. doi:10.1037/a0036065

Giuliani, N. R., & Pfeifer, J. H. (2015). Age-related changes in reappraisal of appetitive cravings during adolescence. *NeuroImage, 108*, 173–181. doi:10.1016/j.neuroimage.2014.12.037

Goldschmidt, A. B., Loth, K. A., MacLehose, R. F., Pisetsky, E. M., Berge, J. M., & Neumark-Sztainer, D. (2015). Overeating with and without loss of control: Associations with weight status, weight-related characteristics, and psychosocial health. *International Journal of Eating Disorders, 48*, 1150–1157. doi:10.1002/eat.22465

Gross, J. J. (1998). Antecedent-and response-focused emotion regulation: Divergent consequences for experience, expression, and physiology. *Journal of Personality and Social Psychology, 74*, 224. doi:10.1037/0022-3514.74.1.224

Gullone, E., & Taffe, J. (2012). The emotion regulation questionnaire for children and adolescents (ERQ-CA): A psychometric evaluation. *Psychological Assessment, 24*, 409–417. doi:10.1037/a0025777

Hilbert, A. (2013). Cognitive-behavioral therapy for binge eating disorder in adolescents: Study protocol for a randomized controlled trial. *Trials, 14*, 312. doi:10.1186/1745-6215-14-312

Hou, F., Xu, S., Zhao, Y., Lu, Q., Zhang, S., Zu, P., ... Tao, F. (2013). Effects of emotional symptoms and life stress on eating behaviors among adolescents. *Appetite, 68*, 63–68. doi:10.1016/j.appet.2013.04.010

Hsieh, H.-F., & Shannon, S. E. (2005). Three approaches to qualitative content analysis. *Qualitative Health Research, 15*, 1277–1288. doi:10.1177/1049732305276687

Hudson, J. I., Hiripi, E., Pope, H. G., Jr., & Kessler, R. C. (2007). The prevalence and correlates of eating disorders in the national comorbidity survey replication. *Biological Psychiatry, 61*, 348–358. doi:10.1016/j.biopsych.2006.03.040

Ivanova, I. V., Tasca, G. A., Hammond, N., Balfour, L., Ritchie, K., Koszycki, D., & Bissada, H. (2015). Negative affect mediates the relationship between interpersonal problems and binge-eating disorder symptoms and psychopathology in a clinical sample: A test of the interpersonal model. *European Eating Disorders Review, 23*, 133–138. doi:10.1002/erv.2344

Kamody, R. C., Thurston, I. B., Pluhar, E. I., Han, J. C., & Burton, E. T. (2019). Implementing a condensed dialectical behavior therapy skills group for binge-eating behaviors in adolescents. *Eating and Weight Disorders, 24*, 367–372. doi:10.1007/s40519-018-0580-4

Kuczmarski, R. J., Ogden, C. L., Guo, S. S., Grummer-Strawn, L. M., Flegal, K. M., Mei, Z., ... Johnson, C. L. (2002). 2000 CDC growth charts for the United States: Methods and development. *Vital and Health Statistics, 11*, 1–190.

Lee-Winn, A. E., Reinblatt, S. P., Mojtabai, R., & Mendelson, T. (2016). Gender and racial/ethnic differences in binge eating symptoms in a nationally representative sample of adolescents in the United States. *Eating Behaviors, 22*, 27–33. doi:10.1016/j.eatbeh.2016.03.021

Lenz, A. S., Taylor, R., Fleming, M., & Serman, N. (2014). Effectiveness of dialectical behavior therapy for treating eating disorders. *Journal of Counseling & Development, 92*, 26–35. doi:10.1002/j.1556-6676.2014.00127.x

Leon, A. C., Davis, L. L., & Kraemer, H. C. (2011). The role and interpretation of pilot studies in clinical research. *Journal of Psychiatric Research, 45*, 626–629. doi:10.1016/j.jpsychires.2010.10.008

Linehan, M. M. (1993a). *Cognitive-behavioral treatment of borderline personality disorder*. New York, NY: Guilford Press.

Linehan, M. M. (1993b). *Skills training manual for treating borderline personality disorder*. New York, NY: Guilford Press.

Linehan, M. M., & Chen, E. Y. (2005). *Dialectical behavior therapy for eating disorders*. New York, NY: Springer.

Malterud, K., Siersma, V. D., & Guassora, A. D. (2015). Sample size in qualitative interview studies: Guided by information power. *Qualitative Health Research, 26*, 1753–1760. doi:10.1177/1049732315617444

Marques, L., Alegria, M., Becker, A. E., Chen, C. N., Fang, A., Chosak, A., & Diniz, J. B. (2011). Comparative prevalence, correlates of impairment, and service utilization for eating disorders across US ethnic groups: Implications for reducing ethnic disparities in health care access for eating disorders. *International Journal of Eating Disorders, 44*, 412–420. doi:10.1002/eat.20787

Masheb, R. M., & Grilo, C. M. (2006). Emotional overeating and its associations with eating disorder psychopathology among overweight patients with binge eating disorder. *International Journal of Eating Disorders, 39*, 141–146. doi:10.1002/eat.20221

McClelland, J., Hodsoll, J., Brown, A., Lang, K., Boysen, E., Flynn, M., … Schmidt, U. (2018). A pilot evaluation of a novel first episode and rapid early intervention service for eating disorders (FREED). *European Eating Disorders Review, 26*, 129–140. doi:10.1002/erv.2579

Memel, B. (2012). A quality improvement project to decrease the length of stay on a psychiatric adolescent partial hospital program. *Journal of Child and Adolescent Psychiatric Nursing, 25*, 207–218. doi:10.1111/jcap.12005

Murray, S. B., Anderson, L. K., Cusack, A., Nakamura, T., Rockwell, R., Griffiths, S., & Kaye, W. H. (2015). Integrating family-based treatment and dialectical behavior therapy for adolescent bulimia nervosa: Preliminary outcomes of an open pilot trial. *Eating Disorders: the Journal of Treatment & Prevention, 23*, 336–344. doi:10.1080/10640266.2015.1044345

Neacsiu, A. D., Rizvi, S. L., Vitaliano, P. P., Lynch, T. R., & Linehan, M. M. (2010). The dialectical behavior therapy ways of coping checklist: Development and psychometric properties. *Journal of Clinical Psychology, 66*, 563–582. doi:10.1002/jclp.20685

Nelson-Gray, R. O., Keane, S. P., Hurst, R. M., Mitchell, J. T., Warburton, J. B., Chok, J. T., & Cobb, A. R. (2006). A modified DBT skills training program for oppositional defiant adolescents: Promising preliminary findings. *Behaviour Research and Therapy, 44*, 1811–1820. doi:10.1016/j.brat.2006.01.004

Nguyen-Rodriguez, S. T., Chou, C.-P., Unger, J. B., & Spruijt-Metz, D. (2008). BMI as a moderator of perceived stress and emotional eating in adolescents. *Eating Behaviors, 9*, 238–246. doi:10.1016/j.eatbeh.2007.09.001

Nock, M. K., Goldman, J. L., Wang, Y., & Albano, A. M. (2004). From science to practice: The flexible use of evidence-based treatments in clinical settings. *Journal of the American Academy Child Adolescent Psychiatry, 43*(6), 777–780. doi:10.1097/01.chi.0000120023.14101.58

Pennell, A., Webb, C., Agar, P., Federici, A., & Couturier, J. (2019). Implementation of dialectical behavior therapy in a day hospital setting for adolescents with eating disorders. *Journal of the Canadian Academy of Child and Adolescent Psychiatry, 28*, 21–29.

Peterson, C. M., Van Diest, A. M. K., Mara, C. A., & Matthews, A. (2019). Dialectical behavioral therapy skills group as an adjunct to family-based therapy in adolescents with restrictive eating disorders. *Eating Disorders: the Journal of Treatment & Prevention, Epub Ahead of Print*, 1–13. doi:10.1080/10640266.2019.1568101

Pluhar, E. I., Kamody, R. C., Sanchez, J., Thurston, I. B., & Burton, E. T. (2018). Description of an intervention to treat binge-eating behaviors among adolescents: Applying the template for intervention descriptions and replication. *International Journal of Eating Disorders, 51*, 1128–1133. doi:doi:10.1002/eat.22954

Polivy, J., & Herman, C. P. (1993). Etiology of binge eating: Psychological mechanisms. In C. G. Fairburn & G. T. Wilson (Eds.), *Binge eating: Nature, assessment, and treatment* (pp. 173–205). New York, NY, US: Guilford Press.

Ricard, R. J., Lerma, E., & Heard, C. C. C. (2013). Piloting a dialectical behavioral therapy (DBT) infused skills group in a disciplinary alternative education program (DAEP). *The Journal for Specialists in Group Work, 38*, 285–306. doi:10.1080/01933922.2013.834402

Safer, D. L., Lock, J., & Couturier, J. L. (2007). Dialectical behavior therapy modified for adolescent binge eating disorder: A case report. *Cognitive and Behavioral Practice, 14*, 157–167. doi:10.1016/j.cbpra.2006.06.001

Safer, D. L., Telch, C. F., & Chen, E. Y. (2009). *Dialectical behavior therapy for binge eating and bulimia*. New York, NY: The Guilford Press.

Salbach-Andrae, H., Bohnekamp, I., Pfeiffer, E., Lehmkuhl, U., & Miller, A. L. (2008). Dialectical behavior therapy of anorexia and bulimia nervosa among adolescents: A case series. *Cognitive and Behavioral Practice, 15*, 415–425. doi:10.1016/j.cbpra.2008.04.001

Schleider, J., & Weisz, J. (2018). A single-session growth mindset intervention for adolescent anxiety and depression: 9-month outcomes of a randomized trial. *Journal of Child Psychology and Psychiatry, 59*, 160–170. doi:10.1111/jcpp.12811

Sellers, R., Caldwell, C., Schmeelk-Cone, K., & Zimmerman, M. (2003). Racial identity, racial discrimination, perceived stress, and psychological distress among African American young adults. *Journal of Health and Social Behavior, 44*, 302–317. Retrieved from www.jstor.org/stable/1519781

Simons, J. S., & Gaher, R. M. (2005). The distress tolerance scale: Development and validation of a self-report measure. *Motivation and Emotion, 29*, 83–102. doi:10.1007/s11031-005-7955-3

Skelton, J. A., & Beech, B. M. (2011). Attrition in paediatric weight management: A review of the literature and new directions. *Obesity Reviews, 12*, e273–e281. doi:10.1111/j.1467-789X.2010.00803.x

Sonneville, K. R., Horton, N. J., Micali, N., Crosby, R. D., Swanson, S. A., Solmi, F., & Field, A. E. (2013). Longitudinal associations between binge eating and overeating and adverse outcomes among adolescents and young adults: Does loss of control matter?. *JAMA Pediatrics, 167*, 149–155. doi:10.1001/2013.jamapediatrics.12

Stice, E., Yokum, S., Burger, K., Rohde, P., Shaw, H., & Gau, J. M. (2015). A pilot randomized trial of a cognitive reappraisal obesity prevention program. *Physiology & Behavior, 138*, 124–132. doi:10.1016/j.physbeh.2014.10.022

Swanson, S. A., Crow, S. J., Le Grange, D., Swendsen, J., & Merikangas, K. R. (2011). Prevalence and correlates of eating disorders in adolescents: Results from the national comorbidity survey replication adolescent supplement. *JAMA Psychiatry (Chicago, Ill.), 68*, 714–723. doi:10.1001/archgenpsychiatry.2011.22

Tanofsky-Kraff, M., Shomaker, L. B., Olsen, C., Roza, C. A., Wolkoff, L. E., Columbo, K. M., ... Yanovski, J. A. (2011). A prospective study of pediatric loss of control eating and psychological outcomes. *Journal of Abnormal Psychology*, *120*, 108–118. doi:10.1037/a0021406

Tanofsky-Kraff, M., Theim, K. R., Yanovski, S. Z., Bassett, A. M., Burns, N. P., Ranzenhofer, L. M., ... Yanovski, J. A. (2007). Validation of the emotional eating scale adapted for use in children and adolescents (EES-C). *International Journal of Eating Disorders*, *40*, 232–240. doi:10.1002/eat.20362

Taylor, J. Y., Caldwell, C. H., Baser, R. E., Faison, N., & Jackson, J. S. (2007). Prevalence of eating disorders among blacks in the national survey of american life. *International Journal of Eating Disorders*, *40*, S10–S144. doi:10.1002/eat.20451

Telch, C. F., Agras, W. S., & Linehan, M. M. (2001). Dialectical behavior therapy for binge eating disorder. *Journal of Consulting and Clinical Psychology*, *69*, 1061. doi:10.1037/0022-006X.69.6.1061

Trace, S. E., Thornton, L. M., Root, T. L., Mazzeo, S. E., Lichtenstein, P., Pedersen, N. L., & Bulik, C. M. (2012). Effects of reducing the frequency and duration criteria for binge eating on lifetime prevalence of bulimia nervosa and binge eating disorder: Implications for DSM-5. *International Journal of Eating Disorders*, *45*, 531–536. doi:10.1002/eat.20955

Udo, T., & Grilo, C. M. (2018). Prevalence and correlates of DSM-5-defined eating disorders in a nationally representative sample of U.S. adults. *Biological Psychiatry*, *84*, 345–354. doi:10.1016/j.biopsych.2018.03.014

Wisniewski, L., & Kelly, E. (2003). The application of dialectical behavior therapy to the treatment of eating disorders. *Cognitive and Behavioral Practice*, *10*, 131–138. doi:10.1016/S1077-7229(03)80021-4

Yokum, S., & Stice, E. (2013). Cognitive regulation of food craving: Effects of three cognitive reappraisal strategies on neural response to palatable foods. *International Journal of Obesity*, *37*, 1565–1570. doi:10.1038/ijo.2013.39

Zapolski, T. C. B., & Smith, G. T. (2017). Pilot study: Implementing a brief DBT skills program in schools to reduce health risk behaviors among early adolescents. *The Journal of School Nursing*, *33*, 198–204. doi:10.1177/1059840516673188

Zhu, H., Luo, X., Cai, T., He, J., Lu, Y., & Wu, S. (2016). Life event stress and binge eating among adolescents: The roles of early maladaptive schemas and impulsivity. *Stress and Health*, *32*, 395–401. doi:10.1002/smi.2634

Dialectical behavior therapy guided self-help for binge-eating disorder

Therese E. Kenny, Jacqueline C. Carter, and Debra L. Safer

ABSTRACT

Binge-eating disorder (BED) is a prevalent and serious public health issue. BED is characterized by recurrent out-of-control binge eating episodes in the absence of extreme weight control behavior and is associated with significant psychosocial and physiological impairment. Dialectical Behavior Therapy (DBT), based on the affect regulation model of binge eating, is an evidence-based treatment (EBT) approach for BED. Unfortunately, access to EBTs is often limited due to geographical barriers (i.e., lack of local providers with specialized training in EBTs), lack of financial resources, and/or time constraints. Self-help approaches (via guided and unguided versions) to delivering DBT for BED offer a potentially effective means of more widely disseminating this treatment. Compared to traditional, higher intensity approaches, self-help DBT for BED is less time-consuming, less financially costly, and requires less need for specialized therapist-training. This paper will present how DBT for BED has been adapted for self-help delivery, review the limited but promising research on DBT self-help available to date, and provide directions for future research.

Clinical Implications

- Dialectical behavior therapy guided self-help shows promise in treating binge-eating disorder
- Dialectical behavior therapy guided self-help is a highly disseminable and cost-effective treatment option
- Dialectical behavior therapy guided self-help may be used within stepped-care approaches to increase treatment availability

Introduction

Binge-eating disorder (BED), characterized by episodes of binge eating in the absence of extreme weight control behavior (American Psychological

Association, 2013), is a prevalent and serious mental health disorder associated with psychosocial and physiological impairment, including elevated rates of psychiatric (Grilo, White, & Masheb, 2009; Hudson, Hiripi, Pope, & Kessler, 2007; Telch & Stice, 1998) and medical morbidity (Cremonini et al., 2009; Mitchell et al., 2015; Succurro et al., 2015; Trace et al., 2012), and deficits in quality of life (Rieger, Wilfley, Stein, Marino, & Crow, 2005; Singleton, Kenny, Hallett, & Carter, 2019).

Dialectical behavior therapy for BED

While Cognitive Behavioral Therapy (CBT; Fairburn, 2008) and Interpersonal Psychotherapy (IPT; Klerman & Weissman, 1993; Wilfley et al., 1993, 2002)—currently the psychotherapeutic interventions for BED with the strongest evidence base—are effective, a significant subset of patients remain symptomatic at post-treatment or follow-up. Such outcomes have been the impetus for the development of other treatment approaches for BED founded upon alternative theoretical models, such as Dialectical Behavior Therapy (DBT). Unlike CBT or IPT, DBT is based on the affect regulation model in which binge eating and other disordered eating patterns are conceptualized as a means, albeit maladaptive in the longer term, of regulating or modulating intense emotions (see, e.g., Haedt-Matt et al., 2014; Waller, 2003; Wiser & Telch, 1999).

Evidence from biological and self-report studies support this model, suggesting that individuals with BED do indeed experience difficulties with ER (Brockmeyer et al., 2014; EiEichen, Chen, Boutelle, & McCloskey, 2017; Harrison, Mitchison, Rieger, Rodgers, & Mond, 2016; Kenny, Singleton, & Carter, 2017; Robinson, Safer, Austin, & Etkin, 2015; Svaldi, Griepenstroh, Tuschen-Caffier, & Ehring, 2012). Moreover, after controlling for body mass index (BMI), age, depressive symptoms, and anxiety symptoms, self-reported difficulties in emotion regulation was the only predictor of the number of binge episodes in the past three months among individuals with BED (Kenny et al., 2017), suggesting an association between the degree of difficulty managing intense emotions and frequency of binge eating. Consequently, Wiser and Telch (1999) have argued that dialectical behavior therapy (DBT) may provide a "toolbox" of emotion regulation skills that could be effective in reducing binge eating and ED pathology in BED.

Though the number of studies investigating DBT adapted for BED are limited, randomized controlled trials comparing group DBT to both a wait-list (Telch, Agras, & Linehan, 2001) and active comparison control (Safer, Robinson, & Jo, 2010) support DBT as an efficacious intervention for adults with BED. For example, post-treatment abstinence rates have ranged from 64–89%, with fairly good maintenance rates of 57–64% at 6–12 month follow-up (Safer et al., 2010; Telch et al., 2001). When compared to non-specialized BED treatment (i.e., active comparison group lacking features specific to DBT and BED), DBT for BED decreases binge eating more quickly (though differences diminish at follow-up), is associated with significantly less drop-out, and shows greater efficacy among patients with increased psychopathology (Robinson & Safer, 2012). Moreover, in a recent randomized controlled trial, Lammers, Vroling, Crosby, and Tatjana (2019) reported that DBT was as effective as CBT in reducing ED and general psychopathology, with half the dosage (i.e., 2 hours per week of DBT vs. 4 hours per week of CBT). Chen et al. (2017) similarly found that DBT and CBT were comparable in reducing objective binge eating episodes among individuals who were early weak responders to CBT-guided self-help. Thus, there is growing evidence for the efficacy of DBT for BED continues to grow, although most studies to date are uncontrolled (see review by Bankoff, Karpel, Forbes, & Pantalone, 2012).

Self-help approaches for BED

Unfortunately, a number of barriers limit the access of patients with BED to specialized treatment for their eating disorder. These include geographical barriers (i.e., lack of local providers with specialized training in evidence-based treatments [EBTs]), lack of financial resources, and/or time constraints. Self-help approaches offer a potentially effective means of bridging this access-to-care gap and broadening treatment availability (Beintner, Jacobi, & Schmidt, 2014). Compared to traditional, higher intensity delivery modes (e.g., face-to-face 50–60 minute individual therapist-led sessions), self-help interventions for BED have the advantages of lower time commitments, lowered expense, and lowered requirements for specialized therapist-training. Of note, self-help can be delivered in (1) a guided format (GSH) in which the self-help materials are augmented by limited contact with a therapist or other health care professional (e.g., nurse) or (2) an unguided self-help format (USH), in which the self-help materials are used independently, without provision of guidance.

Research findings, including systematic reviews and meta-regression analyses (e.g., Beintner et al., 2014; Traviss-Turner, West, & Hill, 2017), demonstrate the effectiveness of both GSH and USH in reducing symptoms of BED. For example, Wilson, Wilfley, Agras, and Bryson (2010) reported that patients with BED who received CBT-GSH achieved similar improvements in binge symptoms (e.g., abstinence rates of approximately 60%) to those who receive traditional, individually-delivered IPT.

Although reviews of self-help treatments for binge eating note considerable outcome variability across studies, likely related to differences in length of treatment and the delivery of guidance via different modalities (e.g., telephone/email/internet/in-person, etc), the generally positive outcomes of CBT-GSH have led to its recommendation as the first-line treatment (as part of a stepped-care approach) for patients with BED according to the latest version of the NICE guidelines (NICE, 2017).

DBT-GSH: rationale and empirical support

Despite the efficacy of CBT-GSH in the study by Wilson et al. (2010), approximately 40% of the patients with BED who received this intervention continued to binge eat at both post-treatment and follow-up. Also, attrition from CBT-GSH was significantly higher (30%) compared to the IPT condition (7%) and moderator analyses revealed CBT-GSH was less effective among patients whose baseline eating disorder symptoms were more severe (Wilson et al., 2010). Expanding the evidence-based interventions available in self-help formats may allow for increased individualization of patient care and improved outcomes, as some patients may show greater improvements with an affect regulation based intervention such as DBT rather than with CBT's dietary restraint-based theoretical model.

Hence, a guided self-help version of DBT was developed from the previously published DBT for BED therapist manual in which patients received 20 two-hour therapist-led face-to-face group sessions (Safer, Telch, & Chen, 2009). In adapting this DBT therapist manual for guided self-help, key changes were made so that the material was more accessible and "digestible" for patients to read on their own either as unguided self-help or with the addition of limited guidance.

The resulting DBT-GSH self-help manual was tested in a randomized controlled study conducted by Masson, von Ranson, Wallace, and Safer (2013). Sixty men and women with BED were randomized to either 13 weeks of DBT-GSH or a wait-list control. Those in DBT-GSH attended one 45-min in-person orientation session in which they received the DBT-GSH Manual (referred to as the "Toolbox") and learned about the basic tenets of DBT treatment. In addition, patients received six biweekly 20-minute support/coaching phone calls over the 13 weeks of treatment. As part of the telephone support, patients were asked a series of standardized questions (See Table 1).

Binge abstinence after 13 weeks was 40% in the intent-to-treat sample and 50% among completers as compared to 3% among the wait-list condition. In terms of binge eating frequency, mean percent reduction in number of binge eating episodes was 2.5 times greater for those in the DBT condition (68%) than patients in the wait-list condition (27%; Masson et al., 2013). Though abstinence rates decreased to 30%, over the 6- month follow-up, Masson et al. (2013) reported that 75% of those initially abstinent in DBT-GSH at post-treatment remained abstinent at follow-up. Greater improvement in self-reported emotion regulation between pre- and post-treatment was found to significantly predict abstinence both at post-treatment and over follow-up (Wallace, Masson, Safer, & von Ranson, 2014).

Table 1. DBT-GSH questions used in Masson et al. (2013).

Questions
1. How have you been doing with your eating since we last spoke?
2. Any questions about the material you read in the Toolbox?
3. What page have you currently read to in the Toolbox?
4. Have you been filling out diary cards every (or almost every) week?
5. Have you been completing chain analyses every (or almost every) week?
6. Since we last spoke, have you found the material in the Toolbox helpful?
a. If so, what in particular?
b. Anything getting in the way of using the Toolbox? [Therapist lists any road blocks preventing patient from working on treatment and possible ways to ameliorate this]
7. This is your ____ check in. In order to complete the treatment in 13 weeks you currently should have read up to Chapter _____.

These findings, though from a small pilot study, appear roughly comparable to previous findings from the CBT-GSH literature. This is even more striking considering that many of the previous GSH interventions were delivered at a greater treatment intensity. For example, Wilson et al. (2010) delivered CBT-GSH in ten 25-minute face-to-face sessions over 6 months compared to six 20-minute telephone calls over 3 months (Masson et al., 2013). This evidence suggests that some individuals are responsive to minimally intensive GSH, allowing for greater treatment reach.

Feedback from participants in the Masson et al. (2013) study was useful in further modifying the DBT-GSH manual so that it contained illustrative case examples, simpler language, discussion of additional topics (e.g., the concept of being "addicted" to food, risks related to dieting, and realistic expectations regarding weight loss). The current updated self-help manual has been published as a self-help book called *The DBT Solution to Emotional Eating* (Safer, Adler, & Masson, 2018).

Using this manual, an innovative study was recently undertaken to examine how technological advances can be harnessed to extend the reach of GSH to patients with BED. The study protocol involved three conditions: 12 weeks of DBT-GSH delivered via video-conferencing, 12 weeks of unguided DBT self-help (DBT-USH), and a 12 week active unguided self-help active comparison control condition (Carter, Kenny, Singleton, Van Wijk, & Heath, under review). In this last condition, the self-help materials did not address binge eating but consisted of a self-help manual focused on CBT techniques to improve self-esteem (SE-USH).

Participants in both DBT conditions were sent a copy of *The DBT Solution to Emotional Eating* (Safer et al., 2018). Participants in all conditions were asked to work through the self-help book at their own pace over 12 weeks, with participants in the DBT-GSH condition also offered six 30-minute video-conference GSH sessions with a graduate student in clinical psychology. Results from this study showed that participants in all groups reported decreases in binge eating, with the greatest decrease observed for the DBT-GSH group (74%) though this was not significantly different from the other groups. Individuals in the DBT-GSH group (25%) were also less likely to meet the frequency criterion for BED in the past month (i.e., four episodes) than those in the SE-USH condition (57%) suggesting greater (and clinically significant) improvement in the DBT-GSH group.

Future directions

Thus far, this paper has described the rationale for adaptation of DBT for BED for self-help delivery and reviewed the limited yet promising research evidence available to date. We now provide directions for future research.

One important area of investigation is examining whether certain moderators of GSH outcome exist. To our knowledge, no studies have yet compared the effectiveness of self-help delivered CBT versus DBT. Even if mean abstinence rates are roughly similar, it is important to investigate whether individuals with certain clinical characteristics would benefit more from the self-help delivery of one versus the other theoretical approach. Ideally future studies would also investigate whether certain individuals may be more responsive to guided versus unguided delivery (potentially irrespective of theoretical approach) and/or to specific delivery mediums (e.g., videoconferencing, telephone, email, text, app). Identifying these kinds of patient characteristics may eventually allow for the development of more streamlined treatments determined by a "brief self-help quiz" at the onset of self-help to provide the reader and/or guided self-help therapist direction regarding some of the previously outlined options (e.g., telephone vs. videoconferencing, CBT vs. DBT). Thus, following preliminary evidence for the effectiveness of DBT-GSH, a logical next line of inquiry would be to examine factors influencing GSH response rates, in order to develop more targeted treatments.

Another fruitful direction for future research is investigating the most effective ways to train therapist or non-specialist "guides" for delivery of DBT-GSH. For instance, DBT—particularly as originally developed for borderline personality disorder (BPD)—has an existing organization (https://behavioraltech.org) focused on issues of training and implementation that could facilitate this important function. Researchers and clinicians may wish to draw from this organization when developing training and implementation strategies. It is important however, to also examine how much (if any) training is necessary for guides. Understanding the amount (if any) and type of training necessary for guides will be important, arguably essential, in making DBT-GSH accessible to non-specialist personnel.

Practical implications

One possible practical application of more research into DBT-GSH and DBT-USH would be a stepped-care DBT approach (e.g., Cornish et al., 2017). At the lowest level of intervention, individuals would receive the DBT self-help book and be asked to work through it on their own. With increasing levels of eating disorder

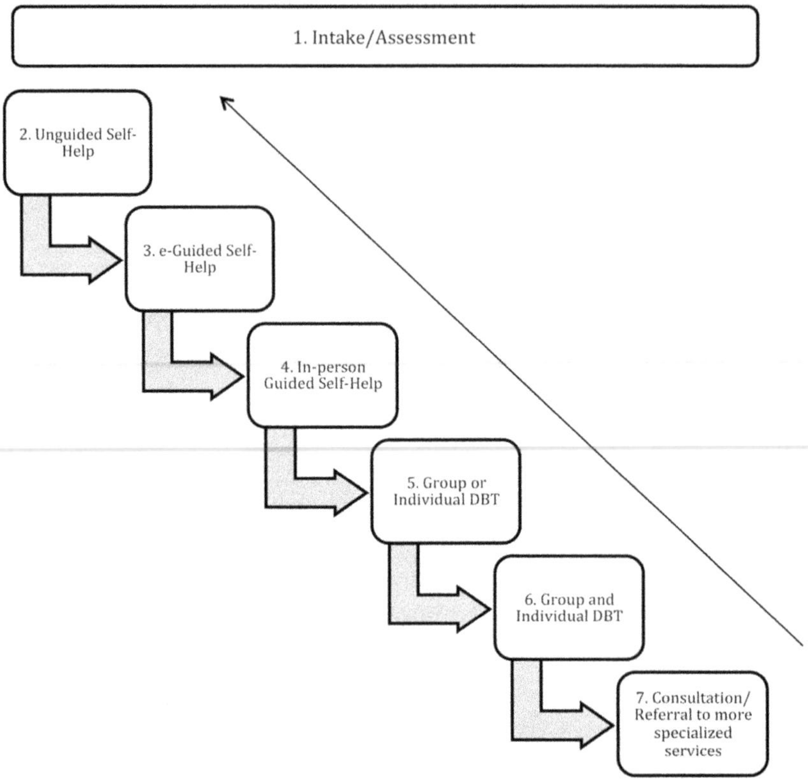

Figure 1. Conceptual illustration of a stepped-care approach to DBT treatment for BED (adapted from Cornish et al., 2017). All individuals enter treatment at Step 1, where they complete an assessment of current BED-related symptoms and psychopathology. Following this, clinicians could direct patients to any of Steps 2–6 (i.e., clients do not need to progress through the steps in order). For instance, individuals who are highly motivated and willing to work on their own may enter at Step 2: Unguided Self-Help. In contrast, individuals experiencing significant distress and report being unable/unwilling to participate in or benefit from self-help may enter at Step 5 (Group or Individual DBT). After clients have entered treatment, their progress can be monitored via clinician assessment. Patients reporting progress (i.e., showing decreases in binge eating and feeling a sense of mastery) may move to a lower step. For example, a patient who entered at Step 4 (In-person guided self-help) may step down to less frequent or shorter e-guided self help sessions. Clients who are still experiencing difficulty or report worsening of symptoms despite time in treatment may move to a higher level of care. For example, an individual who reports no change in binge eating following in-person guided self-help may be stepped up to individual or group DBT. This flexible approach allows clinicians to meet clients where they are and to adapt the level of care based on the patient's response to treatment. As a consequence, treatment is less resource-intensive and more accessible. With more patients potentially entering and leaving treatment more appropriately, hence more efficiently spending their time and financial resources, more clinician time and energy is available for those patients requiring more resource-intensive, specialty-level care.

severity or upon early lack of response to the initial intervention, patients could be assigned to different steps such as GSH via phone or video-conferencing, GSH delivered in person/face-to-face, or more traditional therapist-led sessions of DBT offered individually and/or in group sessions. By monitoring the patient's progress over time, patients can be moved up or down levels accordingly. An example of such a stepped approach is presented in Figure 1. As there is no research on such an approach for BED at present, readers are encouraged to read up on a stepped-care approach before implementing this in their own practice (e.g., Cornish et al., 2017). Moreover, given that the overarching goal of self-help interventions is to make BED treatment more accessible, readers should see the stepped-care approach presented here as one possible means of implementing DBT-GSH. Researchers and clinicians are encouraged to be innovative and creative when implementing DBT-GSH with actual patients. In all cases however, future research will be necessary to evaluate the effectiveness of large-scale implementation of DBT-GSH, including as part of a stepped-care approach.

In summary, the available research evidence points to the potential of GSH as a low-intensity and cost-effective option to bridge the access to care gap for patients with BED in need of evidence-based interventions. There are many barriers for patients wishing to access traditional evidence-based DBT for BED treatment. Dissemination is limited by the requirements for specialized therapist training as well as the fact that treatment, even when available, involves a considerable investment of both time and money. DBT self-help, by providing a more flexible stepped-care approach, may allow more individuals affected by BED to achieve remission and/or recovery without the need for specialized services.

ORCID

Therese E. Kenny http://orcid.org/0000-0002-2659-9408
Debra L. Safer http://orcid.org/0000-0002-9874-2277

References

American Psychological Association. (2013). *Diagnostics and statistical manual* (5th ed.). Arlington, VA: Author.

Bankoff, S. M., Karpel, M. G., Forbes, H. E., & Pantalone, D. W. (2012). A systematic review of dialectical behavior therapy treatment for eating disorders. *Eating Disorders, 20*, 196–215.

Beintner, I., Jacobi, C., & Schmidt, U. H. (2014). Participation and outcome in manualized self-help for bulimia nervosa and binge eating disorder — A systematic review and metaregression analysis. *Clinical Psychology Review, 34*, 158–176. doi:10.1016/j.cpr.2014.01.003

Brockmeyer, T., Skunde, M., Wu, M., Bresslein, E., Rudofsky, G., Herzog, W., & Friedrich, H.-C. (2014). Difficulties in emotion regulation across the spectrum of eating disorders. *Comprehensive Psychiatry, 55*, 565–571.

Carter, J. C., Kenny, T. E., Singleton, C. W., Van Wijk, M., & Heath, O. (under review). Dialectical behavior therapy guided self-help for binge-eating disorder using videoconferencing: A randomized controlled study. *International Journal of Eating Disorders.*

Chen, E. Y., Cacioppo, J., Fettich, K., Gallop, R., McCloskey, M. S., Olino, T., & Zeffiro, T. A. (2017). An adaptive randomized trial of dialectical behavior therapy and cognitive behavior therapy for binge-eating. *Psychological Medicine, 47*, 703–717.

Cornish, P. E., Berry, G., Benton, S., Barros Gomes, P., Johnson, D., Ginsberg, R., … Romano, V. (2017). Meeting the mental health needs of today's college student: Reinventing services through stepped care 2.0. *Psychological Services, 14*, 428–442.

Cremonini, F., Camilleri, M., Clark, M. M., Beebe, T. J., Locke, G. R., Zinsmeister, A. R., … Talley, N. J. (2009). Associations among binge eating behavior patterns and gastrointestinal symptoms: A population-based study. *International Journal of Obesity, 33*, 342–353. doi:10.1038/ijo.2008.272

Eichen, D. M., Chen, E., Boutelle, K. N., & McCloskey, M. S. (2017). Behavioural evidence of emotion dysregulation in binge eaters. *Appetite, 111*, 1–6.

Fairburn, C. G. (2008). *Cognitive behavior therapy and eating disorders*. New York, NY: Guilford Press.

Grilo, C. M., White, M. A., & Masheb, R. M. (2009). DSM-IV psychiatric disorder comorbidity and its correlates in binge eating disorder. *International Journal of Eating Disorders, 42*(3), 228–234. doi:10.1002/eat.20599

Haedt-Matt, A. A., Keel, P. K., Racine, S. E., Burt, S. A., Hu, J. Y., Boker, S., … Klump, K. L. (2014). Do emotional eating urges regulate affect? Concurrent and prospective associations and implications for risk models of binge eating. *International Journal of Eating Disorders, 47*, 874–877.

Harrison, C., Mitchison, D., Rieger, E., Rodgers, B., & Mond, J. (2016). Emotion regulation difficulties in binge eating disorder with and without the overvaluation of weight and shape. *Psychiatry Research, 245*, 436–442.

Hudson, J. I., Hiripi, E., Pope, H. G., & Kessler, R. C. (2007). The prevalence and correlates of eating disorders in the national comorbidity survey replication. *Biological Psychiatry, 61*, 348–358.

Kenny, T. E., Singleton, C., & Carter, J. C. (2017). Testing predictions of the emotion regulation model of binge eating disorder. *International Journal of Eating Disorders, 50*, 1297–1305. doi:10.1002/eat.22787

Klerman, G. L., & Weissman, M. M. (Eds.). (1993). *New applications of interpersonal psychotherapy*. Arlington, VA: American Psychiatric Association.

Lammers, M., Vroling, M., Crosby, R., & Tatjana, V. S. (2019). *Treating binge eating disorder: Dialectical behavior therapy compared to cognitive behavior therapy in a controlled trial.* Paper presented at Eating Disorder Research Society Annual Meeting, Chicago, IL, USA.

Masson, P. C., von Ranson, K. M., Wallace, L. M., & Safer, D. L. (2013). A randomized wait-list controlled pilot study of dialectical behavior therapy guided self-help for binge eating disorder. *Behavior Research and Therapy, 51*, 723–728.

Mitchell, J. E., King, W. C., Pories, W., Wolfe, B., Flum, D. R., Spaniolas, K., … Yanovski, S. (2015). Binge eating disorder and medical comorbidities in bariatric surgery candidates. *International Journal of Eating Disorders, 48*, 471–476. doi:10.1002/eat.22389

NICE. (2017). *Eating disorders: Recognition and treatment* (NICE guidelines CG9). London, UK: Author. Published: 23 May 2017. Retrieved from nice.org.uk/guidance/ng69

Rieger, E., Wilfley, D. E., Stein, R. I., Marino, V., & Crow, S. J. (2005). A comparison of quality of life in obese individuals with and without binge eating disorder. *The International Journal of Eating Disorders, 37*(3), 234–240. doi:10.1002/eat.20101

Robinson, A., Safer, D. L., Austin, J. L., & Etkin, A. (2015). Does implicit emotion regulation in binge eating disorder matter? *Eating Behaviors, 18*, 186–191.

Robinson, A. H., & Safer, D. L. (2012). Moderators of dialectical behavior therapy for binge eating disorder: Results from a randomized controlled trial. *International Journal of Eating Disorders, 45*, 597–602.

Safer, D. L., Adler, S., & Masson, P. C. (2018). *The DBT solution to emotional eating: A proven program to breaking the cycle of bingeing and out-of-control eating*. New York, NY: The Guildford Press.

Safer, D. L., Robinson, A. H., & Jo, B. (2010). Outcome from a randomized controlled trial of group therapy for binge eating disorder: Comparing dialectical behavior therapy adapted for binge eating to an active comparison group therapy. *Behavior Therapy, 41*, 106–120.

Safer, D. L., Telch, C. F., & Chen, E. Y. (2009). *Dialectical behavior therapy for binge eating and bulimia*. New York, NY: The Guildford Press.

Singleton, C. W., Kenny, T. E., Hallett, D., & Carter, J. C. (2019). Depression partially mediates the association between binge eating disorder and health-related quality of life. *Frontiers in Psychology, 10*, 209.

Succurro, E., Segura-Garcia, C., Ruffo, M., Caroleo, M., Rania, M., Aloi, M., … Arturi, F. (2015). Obese patients with a binge eating disorder have an unfavorable metabolic and inflammatory profile. *Medicine, 94*(52), 1–7. doi:10.1097/MD.0000000000002098

Svaldi, J., Griepenstroh, J., Tuschen-Caffier, B., & Ehring, T. (2012). Emotion regulation deficits in eating disorders: A marker of eating pathology or general psychopathology? *Psychiatry Research, 197*, 103–111.

Telch, C. F., Agras, W. S., & Linehan, M. M. (2001). Dialectical behavior therapy for binge eating disorder. *Journal of Consulting and Clinical Psychology, 69*, 1061–1065.

Telch, C. F., & Stice, E. (1998). Psychiatric comorbidity in women with binge eating disorder: Prevalence from a non-treatment seeking sample. *Journal of Consulting and Clinical Psychology, 66*, 768–776.

Trace, S. E., Thornton, L. M., Runfola, C. D., Lichtenstein, P., Pedersen, N. L., & Bulik, C. M. (2012). Sleep problems are associated with binge eating in women. *International Journal of Eating Disorders, 45*, 695–703. doi:10.1002/eat.22003

Traviss-Turner, G. D., West, R. M. &., & Hill, A. J. (2017). Guided self-help for eating disorders: A systematic review and metaregression. *European Eating Disorders Review, 25*, 148–164.

Wallace, L. M., Masson, P. C., Safer, D. L., & von Ranson, K. M. (2014). Change in emotion regulation during the course of treatment predicts abstinence in guided self-help dialectical behavior therapy for binge eating disorder. *Journal of Eating Disorders, 2*, 35.

Waller, G. (2003). The psychology of binge eating. In C. G. Fairburn & K. D. Brownell (Eds.), *Eating disorders and obesity: A comprehensive handbook* (2nd ed. pp. 98–103). New York, NY: Guilford Press.

Wilfley, D. E., Agras, W. S., Telch, C. F., Rossiter, E. M., Schneider, J. A., Cole, A. G., … Raeburn, S. D. (1993). Group cognitive-behavioral therapy and group interpersonal psychotherapy for the nonpurging bulimic individual: A controlled comparison. *Journal of Consulting and Clinical Psychology, 61*, 296–305.

Wilfley, D. E., Welch, R. R., Stein, R. I., Spurrell, E. B., Cohen, L. R., Saelens, B. E., … Matt, G. E. (2002). A randomized comparison of group cognitive behavioral therapy and group interpersonal psychotherapy for the treatment of overweight individuals with binge-eating disorder. *Archives of General Psychiatry, 59*, 713–721.

Wilson, G. T., Wilfley, D. E., Agras, W. S., & Bryson, S. W. (2010). Psychological treatments of binge eating disorder. *Archives of General Psychiatry, 67*, 94–101.

Wiser, S., & Telch, C. F. (1999). Dialectical behavioral therapy for binge-eating disorder. *Journal of Clinical Psychology, 55*, 755–768.

Index

Note: Figures are indicated by *italics*. Tables are indicated by **bold**.

www.ingramcontent.com/pod-product-compliance
Ingram Content Group UK Ltd.
Pitfield, Milton Keynes, MK11 3LW, UK
UKHW050058200926
475702UK00019B/2907
9781003864172